MY LIFE AND TIMES

PREMCHAND

Madan Gopal was born in 1919 at Hansi, Hissar, and educated at CAV High School, Hissar, St Stephen's College, Delhi, and Punjab University. He carved a niche for himself in the world of literary biographies. Considered as 'Premchand's Boswell', he wrote the first ever book on the life and work of Munshi Premchand in 1944, followed, 20 years later, by a full-length literary biography. His translation of Premchand's short stories into English was published as *The Shroud and Twenty-one other Stories of Premchand.* He has also collected and published Premchand's letters in two volumes. According to the *Times Literary Supplement*, 'He has been largely responsible for introducing to Western readers the stories and novels of Premchand.' Authentic, complete and accurate, his books are considered basic source material on Premchand.

A newspaperman for over 18 years, working with the *Civil and Military Gazette*, Lahore, the *Indian Express* and the *Statesman*, Madan Gopal was also a civil servant for 24 years, retiring in 1977, and is the author of over 25 books, including the first book in English on Bharatendu Harischandra, regarded as the father of modern Hindi, the first literary biography of Goswami Tulsi Das, and a novel, *Naye Mode Par*, which has been the subject of intense discussion in Hindi literary circles.

OTHER LOTUS TITLES

Anil Dharker	*Icons: Men & Women Who Shaped Today's India*
Aitzaz Ahsan	*The Indus Saga: The Making of Pakistan*
Ajay Mansingh	*Firaq Gorakhpuri: The Poet of Pain & Ecstasy*
Alam Srinivas	*Women of* Vision: *Nine Business Leaders in Conversation*
Amarinder Singh	*The Last Sunset: The Rise & Fall of the Lahore Durbar*
Aruna Roy	*The RTI Story: Power to the People*
Ashis Ray	*Laid to Rest: The Controversy of Subhas Chandra Bose's Death*
Bertil Falk	*Feroze: The Forgotten Gandhi*
Harinder Baweja (Ed.)	*26/11 Mumbai Attacked*
Harinder Baweja	*A Soldier's Diary: Kargil – The Inside Story*
Ian H. Magedera	*Indian Videshinis: European Women in India*
Kunal Purandare	*Ramakant Achrekar: A Biography*
M.J. Akbar	*Blood Brothers: A Family Saga*
Maj. Gen. Ian Cardozo	*Param Vir: Our Heroes in Battle*
Maj. Gen. Ian Cardozo	*The Sinking of INS Khukri: What Happened in 1971*
Madhu Trehan	*Tehelka as Metaphor*
Manish Pachouly	*The Sheena Bora Case*
Moin Mir	*Surat: Fall of A Port Rise of A Prince Defeat of the East India Company in the House Of Commons*
Monisha Rajesh	*Around India in 80 Trains*
Noorul Hasan	*Meena Kumari: The Poet*
Prateep K. Lahiri	*A Tide in the Affairs of Men: A Public Servant Remembers*
Rajika Bhandari	*The Raj on the Move: Story of the Dak Bungalow*
Ralph Russell	*The Famous Ghalib: The Sound of my Moving Pen*
Rahul Bedi	*The Last Word: Obituaries of 100 Indian who Led Unusual Lives*
R.V. Smith	*Delhi: Unknown Tales of a City*
Salman Akthar	*The Book of Emotions*
Sharmishta Gooptu	*Bengali Cinema: An Other Nation*
Shrabani Basu	*Spy Princess: The Life of Noor Inayat Khan*
Shahrayar Khan	*Bhopal Connections: Vignettes of Royal Rule*
Shantanu Guha Ray	*Mahi: The Story Of India's Most Successful Captain*
S. Hussain Zaidi	*Dongri to Dubai*
Thomas Weber	*Going Native: Gandhi's Relationship with Western Women*
Thomas Weber	*Gandhi at First Sight*
Vaibhav Purandare	*Sachin Tendulkar: A definitive biography*
Vappala Balachandran	*A Life In Shadow: The Secret Story of ACN Nambiar – A Forgotten Anti-Colonial Warrior*
Vir Sanghvi	*Men of Steel: India's Business Leaders in Candid Conversation*

FORTHCOMING TITLES

Lakshmi Subramanian	*Singing Gandhi's India: Music and Sonic Nationalism*
Brij Mohan Bhalla	*Kasturba Gandhi: A Biography*

MY LIFE AND TIMES

PREMCHAND

an autobiographical narrative

recreated from his works by

MADAN GOPAL

LOTUS COLLECTION
ROLI BOOKS

Lotus Collection

First published in 2006
This edition published in 2019

The Lotus Collection
An imprint of
Roli Books Pvt. Ltd
M-75, Greater Kailash II Market, New Delhi 110 048
Phone: ++91 (011) 4068 2000
E-mail: info@rolibooks.com
Website: www.rolibooks.com

Also at Bengaluru, Chennai, & Mumbai

Cover Design: Sneha Pamneja
Production: Lavinia Rao

ISBN: 978-81-7436-432-6

Typeset in AGaramond by Roli Books Pvt. Ltd. and
Printed in India at Repro India Ltd., Mumbai.

AUTHOR'S NOTE

Except for a few passages which are in Premchand's own English – and those in italics – which represent the transcreator's endeavour to fill in the blanks – the entire contents of the pages that follow are an English rendering of Munshi Premchand's own Hindi-Urdu writings.

ONE

I WAS BORN IN SAMWAT, THE HINDU CALENDAR, IN 1937 (1880 AD). I was called Dhanpat Rai. My father was Munshi Ajaiblal, resident of Lamhi village, close to Mahndwa which is situated north of Kashi (Varanashi). I had a sister who was two years older than me. My father was a clerk in the postal department. When I was born he earned about Rs 20 per month. He would be transferred from place to place.

Ajaiblal's elder brother, who had helped get him a job in his own department, died young. So did his nephew. Their families were supported by Ajaiblal, who also got his two brothers jobs in the same department. One of the brothers was convicted and jailed on the charge of embezzlement of funds. He disappeared, not to be seen again. His family was also looked after by Ajaiblal. Ours was a large joint family.

My impressions of my home as a child are just ordinary; neither very happy nor very depressing. I lost my mother when I was in my seventh year. Prior to that my recollections are very hazy; watching my languishing mother who was just as affectionate and, when occasion arose, as stern as all good mothers are.

Of my childhood memories, those of Qazaki are the most vivid. Many years have gone by, yet his figure dances before my inner eye. I was then with my father who was posted in Azamgarh tehsil.

A Passi, Qazaki was bold and full of life and vitality. Every evening he would bring in the mail bag, stay the night, and leave only the following morning. I would wait for him anxiously; at four o'clock in the afternoon, I would go out on to the road and see Qazaki come running with a staff, bells fastened to it, ringing on his shoulder.

He was dark, muscular and hefty. His body seemed to have been cast in a mould with which even the most skilful of sculptors could not find fault. The tiny moustache on his well-formed face created a very pleasing impression. When he saw me, he would quicken his pace; his bells would ring louder and my heart would beat faster. I would run towards him and sit on his shoulders – my throne. Indeed, even paradise dwellers could not have experienced the joy I felt in the movement on Qazaki's powerful shoulders; when he ran with me on his shoulders, it felt as if I were flying on the back of a winged horse. The world would grow small and contemptible.

Qazaki reached the post office, oozing perspiration. But he would not rest. Putting down the mail bag, he would take us children into the fields play with us, sing songs or tell us stories. He knew hundreds of blood-curdling stories of thefts and depredation; of battles, of violence, of ghosts and witches. I would listen and would be overcome with wonder. The thieves and robbers of his stories were heroes who would rob the rich to alleviate the sufferings of the poor. I would admire them.

One day Qazaki was late. The sun was setting, yet there was no sign of him. Like a lost soul I waited. My eyes became sore, squinting to catch a glimpse of Qazaki's familiar figure. I strained my ears, but did not hear the melodious tinkling of his bells. As night fell my hopes faded. I asked everybody coming down the road Qazaki usually did whether they had seen him. Either they would not hear me, or they simply shook their heads. Then suddenly I heard the tinkling of bells. It was dark (and darkness meant ghosts to me; I would forego even the most delicious sweets kept on the shelf in my mother's room if it was dark). But when I heard the tinkling of bells, I ran to meet Qazaki. When I saw him, my anxiety gave way to fury. I beat him, then moved away from him.

'I have brought you something,' said Qazaki laughing. 'However, if you beat me, I won't give it to you.'

'Don't give it to me,' I replied sharply, 'I won't take it anyway.'

'If I show it to you,' said Qazaki, 'you will run and take it in your lap.'

I softened. 'All right,' I said, 'Show it to me.'

'First come and sit on my shoulder,' said Qazaki. 'I am very late today, and Babuji must be very angry with me.'

But I was adamant.

'You show it to me first,' I said. If Qazaki could afford to spare another minute or two, the dice would perhaps have been loaded against me.

He pointed towards something close to his bosom. Its mouth was long, and I could see two sparkling eyes. It was a young deer.

I ran and snatched it from Qazaki's hands. My joy was intense. I have since gone through severe ordeals, attained position and honour, but the happiness which I experienced then has never been equalled. Clutching the young thing I ran home, its soft skin pleasurable. I even forgot that Qazaki had been late that day.

'Where did you find it, Qazaki?' I asked.

'There is a forest,' said Qazaki, 'in which there is a herd of deer. For a long time I have wanted to find a young calf to present to you. Today, at last, I found this little one going along with the herd. I rushed towards it. The herd ran away. The calf also ran. But I didn't give up the chase. While the other members of the herd disappeared, this one was left behind and I caught it. That's why I am late.'

We were still talking when we reached the post office. Babuji saw neither me nor the young deer. His gaze fell on Qazaki. He was furious and shouted at him.

'The dak is already gone! What shall I do with the mail bag now? And where have you been all this time?'

Qazaki did not utter a word.

'Perhaps you no longer wish to continue in this job,' added Babuji. 'Once your bellies are full, you become lazy louts. Starvation alone will teach you a lesson.'

Qazaki still stood silent.

Babuji's temper rose. 'Put the bag down and go home,' he said. You bring the dak at this late hour because you think you stand to lose nothing and that you can earn something wherever you work. But I have to answer for your laziness.'

'I shall never be late again,' said Qazaki, his eyes full of tears.

'Why were you late today?' asked Babuji. 'Answer that first.'

Qazaki still had no answer. I also became tongue-tied.

Babuji, who had to work hard, was easily irritated. That's why I kept away from him. He would come into the house twice a day, for meals, for an hour each. He was busy in office for the rest of the day. He had repeatedly petitioned the officers to give him an assistant but he did not get one and consequently had to work even on holidays. When he got irritated only my mother could calm him. But she could not come to the post office and poor Qazaki was sacked on the spot. His staff, his turban and belt were snatched away from him. He was told peremptorily to quit office.

I wished I had wealth to offer Qazaki and show father that Qazaki was none the worse for his dismissal. Wasn't Qazaki as proud of his belt as a warrior is of his sword?

While Qazaki was taking off his belt, I saw his hands trembling and tears run down his cheeks. The source of all this trouble was the gentle creature which sat with its face hidden in my lap as though I were its mother. Qazaki turned. I followed him. When he reached the door he said, 'It's better for you to go in now. It is very late in the evening.'

Qazaki said again, 'I shall come here to give you joyrides on my back. Babuji has taken away my job, but he will allow me this little pleasure. I won't leave you. Tell your mother that Qazaki is leaving and that she should forgive me for all my faults.'

I went inside and began to weep. Mother, who was in the kitchen, came out and asked, 'What is the matter, son? Who has beaten you? Has your father said something now? I shall question him when he comes. Why does he beat you every now and then? Never go to him again.'

With great difficulty I could utter only one word – 'Qazaki.'

My mother thought that perhaps Qazaki had beaten me. 'Let Qazaki come here today,' she said. 'I shall get him sacked. How dare he, a mere runner, beat my son! I shall have his staff and turban taken away from him.'

'No Qazaki has not beaten me.' I hurried to add, 'Babuji has turned him out. He has taken away his turban and his staff and also his belt.'

'That's worse,' said mother. 'He is a good worker. Why has your father turned him out?'

'He was late today,' I said.

As I put the young deer down (I had no fear of it running away), mother, who had not noticed it until now, was startled. Seeing it frisking about she seized my arm to prevent it from nipping me. I saw my mother's anxiety and, although I had been sobbing bitterly a moment ago, laughed.

'Oh! I see, it is a young deer,' said mother. 'Where did you find it?'

I narrated the whole story as told by Qazaki from the beginning to its terrible end. 'The deer ran so fast, that none other than Qazaki could have caught it. It ran like the wind. Qazaki had to chase it for five to six hours before he caught it. The delay cost him his job and father has also taken away his belt, turban and staff. What will the poor fellow do now except starve?'

'Where is Qazaki?' mother asked me. 'Call him inside.'

'He is standing outside,' I said. 'He asked me to request you, Ammaji, to forgive him for all his faults.'

My mother had until now been treating my story lightly, thinking perhaps that my father had scolded Qazaki mildly. It now occurred to her that Qazaki might have been dismissed. She went outside and shouted for him. But Qazaki was not to be seen. I also shouted for him but Qazaki had left for his home.

I ate my meal, mulling things over. 'If I had money,' I said to myself, 'I would give Qazaki Rs 100,000 and say to him, "never talk to father again". The poor fellow will now have to starve! Would he show up tomorrow? Why should he? But he said he would? I shall make him eat with me tomorrow.' I fell asleep planning.

The following day, I tended to the young deer. The first important thing to do was, of course, the christening ceremony. We named him Munnoo. I introduced him to all my friends and playmates. Before the day was over, Munnoo became attached to me and would follow me everywhere. He acquired an important position in my scheme of things. 'When I build a house,' I said to myself, 'there would be a special room for Munnoo. I also decided I would give him a cot and a carriage to go around in town.'

As evening approached I went out and stood on the road and waited for Qazaki. Although Qazaki had been dismissed, I hoped he would come. It occurred to me that Qazaki may be starving. I ran into the house and while my mother was lighting lamps, I quietly took out a little flour in a basket and ran outside, my hands covered with flour; flour fell from the basket, drawing a line.

I saw Qazaki approach me. He had another staff, a belt round his waist and a turban of his own on his head. The staff had a mail-bag too, dangling from its end. I ran to him, hugged him and asked with surprise where he had got his belt and staff from.

Qazaki lifted me and seated me on his shoulder.

'That belt was no good,' he said. 'It was a badge of servitude. This belt is one of my own liking. Formerly, I served the government. Now I'll serve you.'

While he was talking, he noticed the basket.

'What is this flour for?' he asked.

'I have brought it for you. You must be hungry. Did you eat today?' I replied with some embarrassment.

I could not see Qazaki's eyes, for I was perched on his shoulder. But I guessed from his voice that his throat was choked with emotion. 'My young friend,' he said, 'am I to eat bread only? I need pulses, salt and ghee too. And there is none of these in this basket!'

I felt ashamed of my stupidity. How could the poor fellow eat dry bread? But my mother would now be in the kitchen. How would I bring pulses, salt and ghee for Qazaki? I didn't know it then but my act of theft had been detected; the line of flour had given me away. My mother would not give me the salt, ghee or pulses even if I asked her. Then I remembered that I had a few annas in my school bag; the coppers that I loved to collect had amounted to a few annas.

Although my father never fondled me, he gave me several one paisa coins. Always busy, he may have thought that this was the easiest way of getting rid of me! My mother's temperament was just the opposite. My crying was no obstruction to her work except when she was engaged in accounting, when even my talking loudly was a distraction to her. Although my mother loved me dearly, the very mention of giving me money would make her angry. I had only a few books and some post office forms folded into a book.

'Would all that I have to buy for Qazaki – pulses, salt and ghee – that he needs?' I asked myself.

'Very well,' I said to Qazaki. 'Let me get down from your shoulders. I shall get you the pulses and salt, but will you promise to come here every day?'

'Why shouldn't I come,' said Qazaki, 'if you give me food to eat?'

'I shall give you food everyday,' I said.

I rushed in to the house and brought all my savings for him. 'Then I too shall come everyday,' replied Qazaki.

'Where did you get this money from?' asked Qazaki surprised.

'It is mine,' I replied proudly.

'Your mother will beat you,' said Qazaki. 'She will say: "Qazaki must have persuaded you to give it to him!" Go and buy some sweets for yourself with this money and put the flour back in its pot. I am not starving. My limbs are sound. Why would I starve?'

He would not accept the money I had brought him. He gave me a long ride on his back, sang songs to me and, having brought me back home, he left, putting down the flour basket on our doorstep.

When I went into the house, my mother pounced on me.

'Where did you take the flour to, you thief?' she shouted. 'I see that you are now learning to steal! Tell me, to whom did you give that flour? Otherwise I shall flay you alive.'

I was terrified. When angry my mother was like a lioness.

'I have given it to nobody,' I said, somewhat nonplussed.

'Did you or didn't you take the flour?' asked my mother. 'Look here. The flour is scattered all over the courtyard!'

I was speechless. She threatened me and cajoled me. But I would not open my mouth. My nerves quivered at the thought of the imminent punishment. The flour was at the door! I could go out and bring it in. My faculties appeared to have been paralysed. My feet appeared to have lost the ability to move.

Then all of a sudden I heard Qazaki shouting. 'Bibiji,' he said, 'the flour is at your doorstep. The young one had brought it to give it to me.'

Mother went out of the door. She did not observe purdah for Qazaki. I do not know whether she discussed anything with Qazaki, but she came back into the house with an empty basket, went into her room, took something out of the cash box and returned to the door, her fist closed.

I followed Mother. She called for Qazaki several times, but he had gone.

'Shall I go and look for him,' I asked.

'He was here a moment ago,' she said, closing the door. 'Where will you look for him in the dark? I had asked him to wait until I returned. Yet, he slipped away. He is indeed very shy. Who knows whether he has anything to eat in his house. He wasn't accepting even the flour. With great difficulty I tied it up in his scarf. I sympathize with him. I was going to give him some money. But look at him. He has disappeared.'

I now took courage and narrated the whole story of my theft.

'Why did you not ask me?' asked mother. 'Would I not have given a little flour to Qazaki?'

I did not reply. However, I addressed her in my mind, saying, 'When you sympathize with Qazaki you give him whatever you please! Had I asked you, you would have beaten me. I am pleased, nevertheless, to know that Qazaki won't starve now and that you will give him food everyday and I will get to ride on his back.'

I played with Munnoo. Before dusk, however, I went out and stood on the road. Darkness descended. There was no sign of Qazaki.

The lamps were lit and the road gradually became quiet and deserted.

'Why do you cry, son?' asked mother. 'Hasn't Qazaki come?'

I cried more bitterly. Mother held me to her bosom. It seemed to me that even her voice was choked.

'Be quiet, son,' she said. 'I shall send a runner and call Qazaki tomorrow.' I fell asleep crying. When I awoke the following morning, I asked Mother to call Qazaki.

'I have already sent a man,' said mother. 'Qazaki will soon be here.' I knew that mother always kept her word and satisfied, I started playing.

When I returned home with Munnoo, it was about 10 o'clock. I learnt that Qazaki was not at his house. He had not returned home the previous night. His wife was wondering where he had gone. She had wept. She feared he might have run away.

I felt full of remorse. I didn't know what was troubling me but I felt like crying all the time. I would go outside the house, come back in and go out on to the road again. My eyes were searching for Qazaki. I stood by the roadside like one who was lost in daylight. Suddenly I spotted Qazaki in a lane. I ran after him, but could not reach him. He disappeared. I searched the lane from end to end but there was no sign of him.

I returned home late and when I told Mother what had happened she became worried.

Qazaki was not seen for the next couple of days. I was beginning to forget him.

Another few days went by. One day, when my father was having his meal and I was busy tying brass bells on Munnoo's feet, a woman with a veil appeared. She stood in the courtyard. Her clothes were torn and dirty. But she was pretty.

I went close to her. I asked who she was and what she sold.

'I do not sell anything,' said the woman. 'I have brought these lotus roots for you. I believe you are very fond of them. Aren't you?'

'Let us see,' I said. 'Where have you brought them from?'

'Your runner has sent them for you,' said the woman.

I asked if Qazaki had sent them. The woman nodded affirmatively and began to untie the bundle.

In the meantime mother also came out of the kitchen. The woman touched her feet.

'Are you Qazaki's wife?' asked Mother.

The woman lowered her eyes.

'What is Qazaki doing these days?' asked Mother.

The woman started crying.

'He has been sick, Bahuji, since the day he took flour from your house,' she said. 'He remembers the little one, he cries for Bhaiya. Heaven knows what has come over him, Bahuji! One day, he left home without saying anything and saw Bhaiya hiding in a lane. When Bhaiya saw him, he ran away. He feels embarrassed to come to you.'

'Have you got provisions in the house?' asked mother.

'Yes, Bahuji,' said the woman. 'We have. He got up this morning and went to the tank. He is weak and I implored him not to go out. But he would not listen. His legs were trembling. Yet, he went into the pool and picked up these lotus roots. "Take these lotus roots and give them to Bhaiya," he said. "He is very fond of them. And enquire about his welfare!"'

I had by then taken the lotus roots out of the bundle and was relishing them. My mother frowned at what I was doing.

'Tell him that all is well,' said my mother. 'And also tell him that I too have sent for him.' 'And if he does not come, I shall never speak to him!' I added.

Having finished his meal, Babuji came out and washed his hands. 'Also inform him that Sahib has reinstated him in his job,' he said. 'He should join at once before someone else is hired.'

The woman picked up her piece of cloth and left. My mother called after her. But she would not stop. My mother wanted to give her some provisions.

'Has he truly been reinstated in his job?' asked mother.

'Obviously,' Babuji said, 'I could not send for him on a false pretext, could I? I had recommended his reinstatement five days after dismissing him.'

'It is a good turn that you have done him,' said mother.

'This is the only treatment to cure his laziness,' said Babuji.

The next morning when I got up, I saw Qazaki limping along, supported by his staff. He had become very weak and looked old. The young tree had withered and become just a stump. I ran towards him and hugged him. Qazaki kissed me on the cheeks, tried to lift me to seat me on his shoulders. But he could not bear my weight. He lay on all fours on the ground, like a beast, and I rode on his back to the post office. My joy at that moment was unfathomable.

'Qazaki,' said Babuji. 'You have been reinstated. You must never be late again.'

Qazaki fell down at my father's feet, crying like a child.

I was, however, not destined to have two friendships at a time; when I got Munnoo, I lost Qazaki. Now when Qazaki returned, I lost Munnoo and lost him forever. I still mourn his loss.

Munnoo and I used to eat from the same plate. He would not eat anything unless I shared it with him. He was fond of rice, but would not relish it unless there was a lot of ghee in it. He slept and woke with me. He was so tidy that he would not dirty the house but would go far into the fields to relieve himself. He disliked dogs and would never allow one to enter the house. If he saw a dog, he would leave his food to chase it out.

After leaving Qazaki at the post office, I returned home to have my meal. Munnoo joined me. We had just begun to eat when we saw a hefty dog in the courtyard. Munnoo ran after it.

The dog was the messenger of Munnoo's death. Munnoo chased him into the fields outside without realizing that the fields were not his turf. Inside the house, Munnoo enjoyed his master's support against dogs and he became complacent, overestimating his strength. Now they had reached an area where the dog enjoyed the same rights as Munnoo. The dog pounced on him and broke his neck. Munnoo couldn't even groan.

I heard the clamour of the neighbours and ran out. Munnoo lay dead. The dog was nowhere to be seen.

* * *

I remember my childhood days clearly; the dilapidated mud house, the straw bed, wandering barefoot and barebodied in the fields, and climbing mango trees. The joy I felt in wearing shoes of raw hide is not equalled today when I put on my Flex shoes. The pleasure of drinking fresh and warm sugarcane juice is not rivalled when I now drink rose sherbet nor is the pleasure that I experienced while eating chabena and raw berries equalled when I eat even grapes and khirmohan.

When I was about eight, I used to go with my cousin Balbhadra to the neighbouring village to take lessons from my teacher, a maulvi. Balbhadra was two years older than me. Every morning the two of us would eat the chapattis left overnight, take chabena of peas and barley and leave for the maulvi's school. The day was ours. The maulvi had no attendance register and there was no fine for absence from school. We had no reason to be afraid of anything. Sometimes, we would stop by the police station to watch constables in parade. On other days we would follow the madari as he displayed the pranks of his bear or monkey; sometimes we would make our way to the railway station and watch the trains pass by. We knew the trains' timings like no one else.

On our way to the village school was a garden, patronized by a city merchant. A well in the garden was of great interest to us. The old gardener tending to it would affectionately seat us in his hut. We vied with him to do some of his chores: to water plants with bucketfuls of water, to dig a piece of land with a khurpi, or to prune creepers with scissors. The fun we had! The gardener was adept in child psychology. He would make us work while appearing to oblige us. What would take him a whole day to do, we would finish in a matter of hours.

The gardener is no more. The garden, however, is thriving. When I pass by it I feel like embracing the trees, weeping, and saying to them, 'You have forgotten me but I haven't forgotten you. You are the living picture of selfless love.'

We absented ourselves from school for long periods of time. We would then make such ingenious excuses that the maulvi's taut eyebrows would relax. If I still had the imagination I had then, I would have written a novel which may have become a sensation.

Our maulvi, in fact, was a tailor; he was only incidentally a maulvi. Balbhadra and I would praise the maulvi before the low castes of our village – you could say that we were roving agents for the maulvi. As a result of our efforts, the maulvi would get extra work and we would be very happy. When we had no good excuse to offer for being late, we would take him little gifts: half a seer or so of beans, half a dozen stems of sugarcane or green blades of wheat or barley. The maulvi would see these gifts and his anger would disappear. When these crops were not in season, we would take to other strategems to escape punishment.

The maulvi was a lover of birds. In his school, he had cages for sparrows, shyamas, bulbuls, dahyias and chandolas. We memorized our lessons and the birds learnt them along with us. We would show great enthusiasm in grinding grain for them. The maulvi would also instruct the pupils to catch moths which the birds relished. By sacrificing moths we would placate the maulvi when he was angry.

One morning Balbhadra and I went to the village tank to wash our faces. Balbhadra showed me a shining white object held in his fist. I forced him to open his hand and found he had a rupee coin. Taken aback, I asked him where he had got it from.

'Mother had kept it in a niche,' he said. 'I used the cot as a ladder and took the coin out.'

There was no almirah or box in our house. All the money was therefore placed in a niche high up in the wall. The previous day, my uncle had sold jute and had kept the money, to be paid to the zamindar, in the niche. I don't know how Balbhadra came to know of this. When everyone else in the house was busy with their daily work, he lay the cot on its side, climbed on and took out the rupee.

Until that day we had never touched a rupee coin. Joy and fear surged in my heart. A rupee coin was something beyond our reach.

The maulvi got only twelve annas from us, and he was paid at the end of the month by my uncle personally. We were not trusted, even with this little amount. And that day with the rupee, we were almost kings. Who can ever imagine the pride in our hearts? The only snag in our happiness was the fear of a thrashing. Money in the house was not unlimited and the theft was bound to be detected. Although I had little experience, Balbhadra had been at the receiving end of my uncle's anger. My uncle was an extremely simple man, and if my aunt had not taken steps to harness him, any businessman would have sold him in the marketplace. But when he lost his temper, he would be implacable and even my aunt was scared of confronting him.

My cousin and I conferred about the rupee coin for some minutes. Ultimately, it was decided that now that we had wealth in our grasp, we should not let go of it. We had to ensure that we were not suspected. If we were, we would deny it and say, 'what would we do with a rupee; you can disrobe us and search us.' If we had thought about the matter calmly we might have taken another course of action and would have circumvented the horrible scene that we would have to be part of later.

We returned home and entered the house surreptitiously. Had there been a search at that stage, only God would have been our saviour. But everyone was busy. No one spoke to us. We missed our breakfast, missed even our chabena, took our books and walked to school.

It was the monsoon season. The sky was overcast. Balbhadra and I walked to school supremely happy, happier than what I would have felt if I were made a member of the Council of Ministers. We made a thousand plans, we built a thousand castles in the air. We may not get another chance; we would make the rupee go far. The best sweets in those days could be had at five annas a seer, and the two of us could not eat more than half a seer.

If we ate sweets the rupee would finish. We should therefore eat something tasty, filling and inexpensive. Our eyes felt on guavas. We were delighted. We bought half an anna worth; we got some twelve guavas. Our laps was full. When Balbhadra placed the rupee coin in the hand of Khatikan, the guava-seller, she eyed us with suspicion. 'Where did you get this rupee from, Lala? Have you stolen it?' she asked.

We had a ready answer: we had read at least two or three books, and education had made its impact on us. 'We have to pay the maulvi's fees,' said I, 'and as there was no change in the house, my uncle gave us the rupee.' This reply removed Khatikan's suspicion. The two of us sat on a culvert and ate the guavas with relish. Now we wondered where we would keep the fifteen-and-a-half annas. It was not difficult to hide a rupee coin, but where could we hide a heap of coins? Neither our pockets nor our girdle cloths had enough space. To show the coins was tantamount to announcing the theft. It was decided that twelve annas should be paid to the maulvi and the remaining three-and-a-half annas were to be spent on sweets. Having decided this, we reached school after having been absent for several days.

'Where have you been all these days?' asked the maulvi angrily.

'There was mourning in the house, maulvi saheb,' I said. And while I said this we placed the twelve annas before him. There was no further interrogation. The maulvi was very happy. There were still several days to go before the end of the month, and ordinarily the maulvi got his fees long after the due date and that too after several reminders. To have got the money in advance was a matter of deep satisfaction. We looked at our classfellows with pride in our eyes, as if saying: 'While you fellows do not pay even when asked to, we pay in advance.'

While we were doing our lessons that day, we learnt that there was to be a fair and that we would be let off in the afternoon. The maulvi was also to go to the fair to watch a bulbul fight. Having deposited twelve annas in the bank, we had three-and-a-half annas left and it was decided that this would be our fare for the fair. It would indeed be great fun; we would buy and eat rewrie and golguppa, ride the merry-go-round and then return home in the evening. But the maulvi laid down one stiff condition, namely, that all the pupils must recite their lessons and that those who were not able to do so would not be let off.

Consequently, I got off but Balbhadra was detained. Many pupils also recited their lessons and were allowed to go, and I accompanied them to the fair. As I had the money I did not wait for Balbhadra. It was decided, however, that after he got leave he would also come to the fair and that we would go around the fair together. I promised that I would not spend a single pice until he came. But I did not know that bad luck was in store for me. Even after I had been at the fair for more than an hour there was no sign of Balbhadra. Had the maulvi not given him leave? Or had he lost his way? I looked intently at the road. I did not like going around the fair alone. I also had half a suspicion that the theft had been discovered and uncle had dragged Balbhadra to the house.

When it was evening I bought some rewrie and ate it. Keeping Balbhadra's share of the money carefully in my pocket, I made my way to the house slowly. On the way, it occurred to me that I should get home via the school; maybe Balbhadra was still there. But there was silence in the school. There was one solitary boy there. Seeing me he laughed. 'You'll get a hell of a thrashing when you get home,' he said. 'Your uncle came here and has taken Balbhadra home, beating him all the way; he gave Balbhadra such a blow that Balbhadra fell down. He has been dragged home; and your uncle has got back the fees paid by you to the maulvi. Think of some excuse right now, otherwise you'll get beaten up also.'

I was thoroughly confused. The blood in my veins froze. My feet were heavy, and every step I took was an effort. I prayed to as many gods and goddesses as I could remember and promised each one something; laddoos to some, pedas to others and batase to still others. When I reached the village, I thought of the village deity; only his wishes were supreme. Despite all this, however, my heart beat faster as I reached my house. The sky was overcast, and it looked as if it would burst and fall down. People had abandoned their work and rushed home; even the cattle, their tails up, were making for their sheds. Sparrows also winged their way to their nests. And here was I, making my way slowly, as if there was little strength in my feet. I wished that I could get a high fever, or suffer an injury. Even though I walked slowly I did eventually reach.

Outside our house was a mighty tamarind tree. I hid behind it; when it became dark I would stealthily enter the house and hide myself underneath my mother's bed. I would tell mother the whole story after everyone had gone to sleep. My mother never beat me, and if I made an attempt to weep, she would melt. Any residual anger would have disappeared by morning. If my wishful thinking had been fulfilled, I would escape without the least smear. But it wasn't to be. A boy saw me, and saying my name he entered the house. Now there was no hope for me. I had to go in. A cry escaped my lips, like the wail of an injured dog, struck with fear at the sight of someone else coming towards him. My father sat in the barothe. He had been unwell and had come home on leave. He ate pulse soup and in the evening would pour something out of a bottle into a glass and drink it; it may have been medicine prescribed by an experienced hakim. All the medicines smelt strong and were bitter. But my father relished it. Four or five sick persons of the village would also come to my father and take the medicine for a long time. It was to be taken slowly. It was with great difficulty that they rose to dine.

When I entered the house my father was having his medicine. His group of sick people were also there. Seeing me, my father, his eyes red, asked where I had been all this while.

'Nowhere,' I said almost inaudibly.

'You are now learning ways to steal?' he said to me. 'Speak out now whether you have stolen a rupee or not.'

I could see a sword dangling in front of me. I was dumbstruck.

'Why don't you speak,' asked my father with a booming voice. 'Have you stolen the rupee or not?'

Before I could speak, father, the very picture of anger, his teeth grinding, suddenly got up and advanced towards me, his hands raised. I cried and started weeping; I cried so loud that even my father was taken aback. His raised hand stayed where it was. Perhaps he thought that if I cried so loud before he had hit me, maybe I would fall dead if he actually struck me. When I saw that my artifice had worked, I cried louder. Meanwhile two or three of the group caught hold of my father and signalled to me to get away from there.

But the scene inside the house was more frightening. My blood froze. Balbhadra's two hands had been tied to a pillar. His entire body was covered with dust and he was still breathing hard. He had perhaps been rolling in the courtyard; it looked as if the entire courtyard was wet with his tears. My aunt was rebuking Balbhadra, and my mother was engaged in grinding spices. My aunt was the first one to notice me. 'Here he comes,' she said. 'Did you steal the rupee or did Balbhadra?'

'Balbhadra,' I said without the least hesitation.

'If he stole it,' said mother, 'why didn't you tell someone in the house?'

Balbhadra was accustomed to being beaten up, a few more blows would not make much difference to him. But I had never been beaten up. Three or four blows would have meant the end of me. Didn't Balbhadra try to get me into trouble, otherwise why should my aunt have asked me whether I Balbhadra or had stolen the rupee or Balbhadra. My telling a lie would be justified, I convinced myself.

'Balbhadra had threatened to beat me up if I told anyone.'

'Isn't what I said true?' said my mother. 'I have told you he is not accustomed to stealing. If there were some money he wouldn't even touch it. And yet everyone was making fun of me.'

'When did I say that I would beat you if you tell anyone?' asked Balbhadra.

'There, on the edge of the tank,' I said.

'Mother, that's a lie,' said Balbhadra.

'That's not a lie,' said my aunt to Balbhadra 'That's the truth. You are a liar. Everyone else in the world speaks the truth. You have been proven a thief. If your father had been a government servant, had earned money and brought it home, and if a few people had called him a gentleman, you too would have been taken for a truthful lad. He who was destined to enjoy the sweets has eaten them. You were destined to get only blows.' My aunt untied Balbhadra, and took him inside the room. My mother, by her affectionate rebukes, turned the subject of conversation; otherwise Balbhadra would have been beaten further.

Sitting close to my mother I elicited images of my honesty. My simple-hearted mother thought me to be the image of goodness. She was convinced that the fault was entirely Balbhadra's.

A few minutes later I left the room with gur chabena. Balbhadra too came out eating puffed rice. We sat together and each narrated to the other what had happened. My tale was of happiness; Balbhadra's one of woe. But the end was the same: gur and chabena!

TWO

I HAD ANOTHER COUSIN. HE WAS FIVE YEARS OLDER THAN ME; when I was nine, he was fourteen. However, he was only four classes ahead of me, for even though he had started school at the same age as I had, he apparently did not want to hurry in the matter of academics. He believed in a sound foundation and therefore spent two years instead of one in each class. But that he came into the world earlier than I did gave him the right to boss over me.

He was the studious type. One seldom saw him without a book. The only time he rested his brain was when he was drawing pictures of sparrows, dogs and cats in the margins of his books. Sometimes he wrote meaningless sentences on them, or repeated a name ten times. I always wondered why he did that, but could never summon enough courage to ask him. After all he was in the ninth class, and I was only in the fifth. For me to even try and fathom the meaning of what he wrote would be considered impertinence.

I could never put my heart into my studies for long. To read continuously even for an hour was an ordeal for me. At the first opportunity I would try and get out onto the playing fields. But the joy of play was always marred by my cousin. The moment I returned, he would ask, 'Where have you been?' I could never say that I was out playing. My silence would be taken as proof of my guilt. My cousin started his usual elder-brother lecture: 'If it were easy to learn English, everyone would have learnt it. It needs all your sweat and toil. Look at me. Have you ever seen me going out? I devote all my time to my studies. And even then it takes me two to three years to get through a class. You, with your habits, will never be able to pass. If you are so fond of playing, why don't you go home and play? Why waste your father's hard-earned money?'

Sometimes I'd start weeping at his reprimands. I even wondered if he was right, about my wasting my father's hard-earned money. Sometimes, it led to my resolve to mend my ways. A fresh timetable would be drawn up and time allocated to each subject according to its importance. But drawing up a timetable was quite different from working according to it. Within a couple of days the enthusiasm would wear off and my old habit of playing would get hold of me again. The open air, the green fields and the feeling of being alive and independent which the fields always inspired in me was irresistible. This would start afresh the cycle of my brother's advice and reprimands. Consequently I tried to avoid even his shadow. Even my entry into his room was made as noiselessly as possible, so that I might avoid attracting his attention.

The examinations came around. While my cousin failed, I passed. Not only did I pass but also got a first division. There was now a difference of only two classes between us. I felt like telling him what I thought of him and his lectures but he was so crestfallen that I felt ashamed of myself for even having thought such a thing.

The examination results were so encouraging that I started devoting more time to playing. One day when I returned after spending practically the whole morning out, my cousin called me and said, 'I see that your success in the examination has turned your head. But let me warn you that pride destroys one. It has brought down even the mightiest of monarchs to their knees. Think of Ravan. Have you learnt any lessons from his life? The mere passing of examinations is not enough, my boy. One must learn lessons from history. Ravan was so powerful, that even the gods were afraid of him. Power turned his head and he started considering himself greater than the Almighty. And look what his pride did to him. It brought him to an ignominious end. The same fate has befallen many others who were proud like him. You have only had one success so far and you think no end of yourself. One success can be a chance occurrence. Don't think that just because I have failed I have no right to tell you all this. When you come to my class you will know how difficult it is to get through the ninth class. There is algebra to be learnt, and geometry and English history. They have dozens of Henrys and scores of Williams. It is a regular rigmarole. There must be an acute shortage of names among these wretched people that they invented this queer system of first, second, third, etc., to differentiate between their kings. It is no joke to remember what event took place in which Henry's reign. And the moment you write Henry the Eighth, instead of Henry the Seventh, you can rest assured that you will not get a single mark. And geometry. Oh, geometry is really a devil of a subject. If you write ACB instead of ABC, you've had it. I want to ask these examiners what difference it makes after all. Take English compositions. Some stupid examiner would ask for an essay on punctuality which should not be less than four pages, four foolscap pages, mind you. Getting through the ninth class is really hard, I can assure you. Even though I have failed, I know better. Take my advice and don't waste your time, otherwise you will repent.'

I listened to him patiently but these lectures were so often replicated that they had lost their charm for me. The school bell, thank God, came to my rescue and I disappeared. I said to myself, 'This is the result when I have passed. God alone knows what would have happened if I had failed.' The gruesome picture he painted of the ninth class really shook me.

In spite of my cousin's lectures my ways did not change. I worked only when it was absolutely necessary, the rest of the time I played.

The examinations came again. The previous year's luck held my hand. My cousin failed again. And this time he had worked very hard indeed. He used to study till 10 o'clock almost every night and get up at four in the mornings. When the results were declared he started crying. I could hardly control my own tears.

Now there is a difference of only one class between us. I wondered if he would fail again. An unkind thought, I must admit, but then he would not be able to lecture me any more. I spurned the thought spontaneously. Who knows, it may be his constant goading which makes me study and pass.

After his last failure, my cousin softened considerably. Even when he got the opportunity to rebuke me he let it pass. His leniency resulted in greater freedom for me, and I devoted even less time to studies now. A new sport attracted my attention. I started flying kites. Practically the whole day was spent in either their pursuit or in flying them. But I still feared my cousin's outbursts. I flew kites stealthily, without his knowledge.

One evening I was following a kite far away from the hostel when I suddenly saw him. Seeing me running after the kite like a demented dog he caught hold of my hand and said angrily, 'You ought to be ashamed of yourself, running like this with street urchins. Have you no self-respect? I am five years older than you and even if you were to come into the ninth class, with me, I would still be older. Not even God can remove this difference between our ages. Even if you were to pass your B.A. I would still be older than you. Listen, my boy,' he said, 'not all the books in the world can teach what experience teaches. Look at your mother. She has never been to a school. Your father did not go beyond the fifth class. Can you and I ever hope to attain their wisdom? They may not know what type of government America has or how many times Henry the Eighth married, or how many stars there are in the firmament, but there are other more important things that they do know, things one learns from experience alone. If you were to fall ill today, your mother or father would try to diagnose the disease or call a doctor. They would not lose their bearings as you and I would. Don't forget that father has raised a family of nine and spent a major portion of his life on half of what we spend in school today.

I felt ashamed of myself for having given him the impression that I did not care for him any longer and said with great humility, 'You are right in what you say. I shall try my best to come up to your expectations.'

My cousin clasped me tightly in his arms. Tears rolled down his cheeks. 'I do not want to stop you from flying kites,' he said. 'I want to fly them myself. But if I do it myself how will I be able to stop you from doing so? And if I don't stop you I shall be failing in my duty towards you.'

Just then a kite passed over our heads. It had a long string. My cousin jumped, up caught it and ran towards the hostel. I followed him.

THREE

A MEMORABLE EVENT DURING MY CHILDHOOD WAS THE Ramleela, the *Ramayana* staged. I would wait enthusiastically for the Ramleela. It was really an obsession. The venue of the Ramleela was close to my house. And the house where the artistes of the Ramleela had their make-up done was adjacent to my house.

The make-up of the artistes would start at 2 p.m. I would go there and run errands eagerly. Rajkumari's make-up was done in one room. Her body would be plastered with Ramraj paste, her face powdered. Over the powder red, green and blue coloured spots would be painted. The spots would brighten her forehead, eyebrows, cheeks, and chin. The job was done by only one man. It was my assignment to handle the small earthenware pot containing the coloured Ramraj and I would also fan the artistes. After this, the carriage would start moving. I would sit at the back with

Ramchander and be suffused with joy, pride and romance. I felt as if I were in heaven.

On the day Nishad's boat crossed the river, I was lured by boys playing gulli–danda, and missed the make-up session. The Ramleela procession started, but I did not give up the game. It was my turn to play. If it had been the other person's turn to play I would perhaps have run away. But there is great satisfaction in tiring out the opponent. Once my turn was over I ran towards the river bank. The carriage had reached the riverbank. I saw the boatman about to sail away. I ran fast.

But the crowd was thick, and it was not easy to reach the procession. By the time I was able to make my way through the crowd and reach the riverbank, I saw that Nishad had untied the knot holding the boat and sailed away. And Ramchander, whom I taught at the cost of my own studies lest he fail, looked away as if he did not know me.

I pushed my way to the riverbank. Most of the people were preoccupied with their own affairs. They did not hear my wails. I have faced many troubles, but the misery I felt that day has never been repeated. Despite this, when his carriage came nearer, I climbed in.

Ramleela over, Ramchander's coronation was to take place. As the collections made on the occasion of Ramleela were much lower than expected, nobody paid much attention to Ramchander. He wasn't bid goodbye. Nor were any arrangements made to give him a meal. Nobody bothered to give him even water. Despite this treatment, my faith in Ramchander was undiminished. In my eyes, he still was Ramchander. Whenever I had some eatables, I would run to the chaupal and give them to him. The pleasure I got in feeding him was much more than what I would feel if I ate the food myself. If Ramchander was not there, I would look for him and until I made him eat something, I would be restless.

On the coronation day, a huge shamiana came up at the venue of Ramleela. It was very well decorated. Nautch girls also came to perform. In the evening, Ramchander was taken out in a procession which would stop at the entrance of each house. Aarti would be performed for Ramchander. Every householder donated money commensurate with his means. Although my father, because of his official position, did the aarti, he did not pay any donation. At that time, I had a rupee in my pocket which an uncle had given me when he visited us just before Dussehra. I had kept it aside and not spent it even on Dussehra day. I took out this coin, advanced and put it in the tray. Father looked at me with disdain. He said nothing, but pulled a face which suggested that he did not like what I was doing.

By 10 o'clock the procession had ended. The aarti tray was full with cash. I cannot say how much the cash was but it certainly was not less than Rs 400–500. The organizer of the Ramleela had spent more than this amount and was keen that at least another Rs 200 be raised. He decided to raise this amount with the help of nautch girls.

Chaudhary Saheb, the organizer, conferred with the chief nautch girl Aabaadijan. He thought that I was too young to realize what was being discussed but I understood everything.

Aabaadijan would catch hold of people's wrists and practise such coquetry that everyone would dole out some money. Aabaadijan was young, pretty, sexy and provocative. Her movements were enticing. She would correctly assess the worth of each man; no one paid her less than Rs 5. When she sat facing my father, I felt embarrassed. I saw her holding his wrist. I was certain that father would tick her off. But his eyes betrayed lust. I saw father smiling under his moustache. I had never seen such a depraved smile on his face. He freed his wrist. I felt as if my honour had been salvaged. Then she put her arms around his neck. I had thought my father would push this shameless wretch aside. Someone said, 'Aabaadijan, your efforts won't succeed here. Go to someone else.' Father looked at this person angrily and twitched his moustache. He did not say anything, but the expression on his face seemed to say, 'What do you think of me, you miserly fellow. On an occasion like this, I can do anything and what's money anyway? You can try your best. If I don't pay twice as much as you do, I won't show my face.' And then, surprise of all surprises, I saw my father putting his hand in his pocket. He took out a gold coin, showed it to Sethji and gave it to Aabaadijan. There was a big applause. I could have died of shame. Sethji had been humbled. I could see a glow of happiness on the face of my father, as if he had outrivaled Hatim Tai. My father had shown his displeasure when I donated a rupee coin into the aarti tray; my noble act had disgraced him and he was so proud of his dealing with this shameless and fallen creature indulging in this horrible trade. Aabaadijan gave a sweet smile, bade him goodbye and moved to the next person. If I had not been a witness to all this I would never have believed anyone who had told me what had happened.

Whenever I saw or heard of such despicable things, I would report them to my mother. But this time I did not tell her about the incident because I knew it would hurt her.

Singing continued into the night. I could hear the tabla and wanted to go in but did not have the heart to; if someone had narrated what my father had done, what would I have said to him.

Next morning was scheduled for saying goodbye to Ramchander. Rubbing my eyes, I rushed to the chaupal. I was apprehensive, wondering if Ramchander had already left. But when I reached there, I saw that the nautch girls were about to depart. Scores of people, with lust in their eyes, were surrounding them. I went straight to Ramchander. Laxman and Sita were crying and Ramchander, with the trappings of a sadhu slung on his shoulders, was trying to console them. No one else was there. In a hoarse voice, I asked Ramchander, 'Have they bade you goodbye?'

'Yes,' said Ramchander. 'We have been bidden goodbye. Chaudhary Saheb has told us to go.'

'Have you been paid and given the customary clothing?' I asked him.

'Not yet,' said Ramchander. 'Chaudhary Saheb said there was no money left. He told us to come later.'

'You mean to say that you got nothing at all?'

'Not a paisa,' said Ramchander, 'He says there was no saving. I would have bought books with the money. But he has paid us nothing, not even the fare. He said, "Your place is not far away, and you can certainly walk down."'

I felt so angry that I thought of going to the Chaudhary to take him to task and saying to him, 'You pay the nautch girls in cash and you pay them for transport too and pay nothing at all to poor Ramchander and his colleagues. And those people who had showered Rs 10 or 20 cannot spare even two annas, or four annas for these poor souls!'

'Father had given a gold sovereign to Aabaadijan,' I said to myself. 'Let me see how much he gives to these artistes.' I ran to father. He was ready to leave for inspection work.

'Why are you loitering about?' he asked me.

'I had gone to the chaupal,' I said. 'Ramchander is being bidden goodbye, but Chaudhary Saheb has given him nothing. How will they go home?' I said. 'They do not have money even to travel.'

'Haven't they been paid travel expenses?' asked father.

'No.'

'That is unfair of Chaudhary Saheb.'

'If you give Rs 2,' I said, 'I shall give it to him...They may then reach their homes.'

Father gave me a stern look. 'Go and pick up your books. I have no money,' he said

My faith in, and respect for, my father was gone. After that I never paid heed to his orders or his reprimands. 'You don't have any right to give me sermons or to preach to me,' I said in my heart. I started hating the very sight of him. I would act contrarily to what he wanted me to do. This decision, in the end, has harmed me but at that time my heart was full of rebellious thoughts.

I had saved two annas which were still with me. I quietly took them out and went and gave them to Ramchander. The joy with which he received the money was beyond my expectation. It was as if a thirsty man was getting water. With only two annas, the artistes of the Ramleela bade goodbye. Only I went to see them off.

When I returned home after waving them off, my eyes were wet but my heart was full of joy and happiness.

FOUR

ONCE MY MOTHER'S FATHER WAS ILL AND MY MOTHER WAS sent for. She was away for three months. As I had to sit for my examinations, I did not accompany her. During the three months she was away, I polished off forty seers of gur in addition to some more that she had left for me to eat in a smaller earthen pitcher. The forty seers of gur had been stored in a bigger pitcher which was covered with an earthen lid and sealed with mud plaster. She had given me strict instructions not to break the seal. I ate the gur she had left for me on Sundays. I ate gur in the morning, I ate gur with bread in the afternoon, gur with dry gram in the evening and gur with milk at night; my mother would not have objected to this. I would also quietly leave school, come home on the pretext of drinking water, and take out two or three round lumps of gur to eat. In fact, eating gur became an obsession with me. My coming home meant a dent in the stock of gur. Within a week the small pitcher was empty.

I had been instructed by mother not to open the bigger pitcher containing gur. After a week of her absence, when she was not due back for eleven weeks, it was with great difficulty that I passed a whole day without eating gur. My patience ran dry and, with a sense of guilt, I opened the pitcher. I took out some lumps to refill the smaller pitcher and closed it, determined that it would last for three months, even as I pretended that the bigger pitcher was like the seventh stage which the legendary Rustam could not reach. To make it last for three months was not easy. Like a sweetmeat seller I rearranged the lumps as one trading in matchboxes does with his wares. Thus, even though some lumps had been taken out, it looked like the pitcher was full. Mother would not get suspicious and there would be no occasion to dilate on the subject.

The tastebuds took precedence. My tongue, just a few inches long, was making my heart, a giant, dance to its tune. It was like a madari making a monkey dance.

I had decided several times that I would not eat more than five lumps in a day. This was like the resolve of an alcoholic, and I would curse and tell myself that I was eating too much gur and that during the ensuing monsoon season my body would have sores. I would have to apply a stinking sulphur ointment. No one would want to be next to me.

I would swear by my mother, my future education, my father, cows and God, but then I would forget all about the vows. By the end of the following week this pitcher would also be empty. Then I would pray devoutly to God: 'This greedy restless heart of mine is playing havoc with me. Please give me the strength to overcome it. Give me a strong resolve that I may eschew gur. This wretched thing is compelling me to get a beating from my mother. If you protect me O God,' I would pray, 'I shall survive.'

But God also forsook me and the second pitcher was soon emptied.

Soon after, I had three consecutive holidays and went to be with my mother. She asked me, 'Have you been taking care of the earthen pitcher of gur? I do hope that ants have not entered it or dampness affected it.' I swore by the earthen pitcher and said I had seen there was no dampness nor ants. This obviously worked as proof of my honesty. My mother looked at me with pride for complying with her instructions and told me to refill the small pitcher of gur for myself. She also told me that I should put back the lid with great care.

After hearing her instructions, time began to hang heavy on me. Every minute was like an era. After I returned from my grandfather's home the first thing I did was to open the pitcher and take out a handful of lumps of gur. I ate five lumps at one go and then started the process of polishing off the remaining gur. With mother's permission there were to be no qualms of conscience. The next eight days saw the end of the pitcher's contents.

To overcome my weakness, I put a lock on the room with the pitcher of gur and put the key in the small hole in the wall. How can you get the gur now, I asked myself. To get the key from the hole meant digging deep, nine feet of the wall. And this degree of hard work and courage was beyond me. Within the next three days, my cup of patience was full and a restlessness seized me. Whenever I passed by the side of the room where the gur was kept, I would look towards it impatiently. I clutched at the lock, shook it, but the wretched thing did not give way. I went to examine the hole in the wall, looked deep into it, and tried to gauge its depth with the help of a stick. But I could not fathom its depth. I had lost interest in food and even games. The greed in me tried to argue with, and persuade, the heart to yield. 'After all what is the gur there for, but to be eaten. I am only eating it. How does it matter if I eat it now or later? What right does mother have to stop me from what is not wrong. I don't obey her when she forbids me from going to play or tells me not to climb trees or swim in the village tank, or not to use the bamboo pole to remove sparrows' nests? Don't I have some rights too? Why then should I sacrifice my wishes at her bidding?'

My greed eventually got the better of me. I got up in the morning, took a shovel and started pulling down the wall. There was already a hole in it. It did not take very long. After half an hour of hard labour, a large block, some yards long and three inches wide, fell down and at the bottom of the hole lay the key to success. I took it out, opened the lock and filled the smaller pitcher with gur, and then closed the door to the room. There was now some empty place in the pitcher. In spite of my efforts at rearrangement, the gap could not be filled. And to ensure that I didn't try to fill it till my mother's return, I threw the key into the well. How I broke the lock later and threw its parts into the well when my mother returned and how I reported to her the theft of the gur in the pitcher is another story.

When I was seven years old my mother, who had been bedridden for several months in Allahabad, died. Then my father also fell sick, took leave and was in Lamhi. There he got orders trensferring him to Jeemanpur. My grandmother and I accompanied him there, when he reported duty. There, after a year and half, he, now 48, to my grandmother's dismay got remarried. Grandmother and I returned to Lamhi and I joined a school at Banaras.

FIVE

My anglicized friends may not agree, but I will say that gulli–danda is the king of all games. When I see young boys playing gulli–danda, I feel like joining them. You don't require a lawn for this game nor a court nor net. You just cut the branch of a tree, make a gulli out of it and if there are two people, one can start the game.

The greatest drawback of a Western game is that its equipment is very expensive. Unless you shell out a great deal of money, you cannot be a member of a team. It is only the game of gulli–danda that you can play without any investment. But our people are so enamoured of English goods that we are apathetic to our own things. In our school, a minimum of Rs 3 or 4 is charged every year from each student in the name of sport. No one ever thinks of popularizing Indian games which can be played without any investment. British games are only for the rich. Why burden poor students with these games? There is also no danger in our games unlike in cricket where a ball can injure your head or your spleen or your legs. A gulli can certainly cause a scar on the forehead, but there are many cricketers who have had to take up crutches.

I cherish the memory of going out early in the morning, climbing trees to cut a branch and making a gulli and danda out of it, the enthusiasm of the players, of tiring out the adversary or getting tired out or of those simple squabbles which do not take into account differences in caste or wealth. There is no place here for a show of wealth or false pride.

Mother's domain ends at the entrance to the house. According to her, my future, like a leaking boat, is uncertain. While I am engrossed in tiring out my adversaries, I am completely oblivious of the daily routine of bathing and eating.

The gulli is a tiny thing but it has the sweetness of all the candies in the world. Just the sight of a gulli gives me great joy.

Among my playmates was a boy named Gaya. He was older than me by two or three years. Slim and tall, he had monkey-like long and thin fingers, as also the agility and restlessness of a monkey. He would catch the gulli like a lizard pouncing on insects. I don't know whether his parents were alive, or where he lived and where he ate his meals. But he was the champion of our gulli–danda club. And the team he joined always won. Whenever we saw him coming we would rush forward to welcome him and enlist him for our team.

One day Gaya and I were the only two playing the game. He was fielding and I tiring out. It is strange that one is really very happy tiring out the opponent, but being tired ourself even for a few minutes is irksome. I tried every trick but Gaya was not going to give up without putting me down. I ran towards my house. Gaya chased me, caught up with me and told me sternly to complete the game.

'You mean,' I said, 'that you will tire me out the whole day and I do all your bidding?'

'Yes you will have to play all day,' said Gaya.

'You mean that I have to forego my meals and drinks?' I asked.

'Yes, you will have to,' said Gaya. 'You will not go till my turn is over.'

'Am I your slave?'

'How can you go home? Is this a joke?' he continued. 'You have to play the game. You had your turn. It is now my turn.'

'All right,' I said, 'I had given you one guava yesterday. Please return that to me.'

'That is now inside me.'

'Then take it out. Why did you eat it?'

'You gave it to me, and I ate it. I did not ask for it.'

'As long as you do not return my guava I cannot play,' I retorted.

I had thought justice was in my favour. After all I had given him the guava with some motive. Even alms are given with some motive. Since Gaya had eaten the guava that I had given him, he was obliged to exempt me from completing the game. Guavas, incidentally, were quite expensive; five pieces cost a paisa. Even his father could not afford to eat guavas. This indeed was grave injustice to me.

Gaya pulled me to his side and said, 'You have to play the turn due to me. Forget about guavas.'

Gaya was adamant, I thought, about getting something entirely unjustly. I decided to release myself from his grip. But he would not let me go. I called him names. He slapped me twice. I bit him. He struck the danda on my back. I cried. Gaya could not cope with the situation and ran away. I wiped my tears, forgot the hurt in my back and reached home smiling.

Shortly thereafter, my father got transferred to another place. I was happy to be going to a new place and did not at all feel sorry to leave my schoolmates and friends. But my father was unhappy, because the place he was leaving was good from a pecuniary point of view. My mother too was unhappy because the old place was cheaper for basic necessities and she also had a lot of friends who were like members of the family. But I was happy to be in a new place. There were many tall stately buildings here. If a teacher in the British school here beat a boy he could be convicted and sent to jail. The glances and reactions of boys in the school were an indication of the esteem in which they held me. Indeed, those whom I left behind in the old school must be really envious of me. They seemed to say to me, 'You're lucky you can move on but we have to live in this wilderness and die here too.'

Twenty years later, when I had become a senior officer in the government service, and visited the old place for inspection, I stayed in the Dak Bungalow. Seeing this place, old memories were rekindled. I took my walking stick and started for the township. Like a tired traveller I looked anxiously for the place where I had played as a child. I thought of my playmates. Except for Gaya, I could not recall any other name. In place of the wilderness there once was, there now stood imposing buildings. In place of the bargad tree, was now a beautiful park. The entire place had undergone a transformation. If I had not known the location, I would hardly have recognized it. Memories of childhood friends and playmates revived.

Two or three boys playing gulli–danda caught my attention. For a moment, I forgot that I was a senior government officer with the trappings of the powers vested in me. I went to the boys and said to one of them, 'Son, is there someone with the name of Gaya living here?'

One boy laid aside his gulli–danda and said, 'Which Gaya, Gaya chamar?'

'Yes,' I said casually, 'perhaps the same person; for if there is a person with the name of Gaya, it may be him.'

'Yes,' he said, 'there is one with that name.'

'Can you call him?' I asked.

The boy ran and I saw him bring along with him a tall, black giant of a man. I recognized him even from the distance. I felt like rushing forward, meeting him and hugging him, but I restrained myself and just said, 'Hello Gaya, do you recognize me?'

Gaya bent and said, 'Why shouldn't I recognize you. And how are you?'

'I am the syce of the deputy commissioner,' said Gaya.

'Where is Mohan?' I asked. 'And Durga and Matai? Any news of them?'

'Matai is no more,' said Gaya. 'Mohan and Durga are now postmen. And how are you? You were always bright,' said Gaya.

'Do you play gulli–danda sometimes?' I asked.

Gaya looked at me questioningly. 'Not any more,' he said. 'The struggle for a livelihood does not leave me any time for games.'

'Come,' I said, 'let's play today. You play first, tire me out… You take your turn today.'

It was with great difficulty that Gaya agreed to play. He felt embarrassed. Although I was embarrassed too, mostly because those watching would be amused, I could not have gone away without having had a game with Gaya.

It was decided, therefore, that the two of us would go to a secluded spot to relive the joy of our childhood. I brought Gaya along with me to the Dak Bungalow. The two of us got into the car. I drove to a place where we could play gulli–danda. We also took an axe with us. I was serious, but Gaya thought I was joking. There was no sign of keenness or joy from him.

'Did you ever think of me?' I asked Gaya. 'Tell me the truth.'

'How could I think of you, master,' said Gaya. 'What is my status in life? It was my good fortune to have played with you. I am a nobody now.'

'But I have always remembered you,' I said. 'I remember the danda with which you hit my back. Have you forgotten that?'

'That was foolish of me,' said Gaya, regretfully, 'and don't remind me of it.'

'Why, that is one of my fondest memories of my childhood. The joy I felt when you hit me is more than what I feel when I am honoured now. Such was my joy that even today I recall it with great happiness.'

We had driven about three miles from the township. It was all quiet there. Towards the western side there was a stretch of water where we used to come as children to pick lotus flowers to stick behind our ears.

Dusk was descending. I climbed a tree and broke a branch. This was turned into a gulli and danda. The game started. I put the gulli on the hole and hit it high. It passed by Gaya. He stretched his hand to catch it, but the gulli fell behind him. He used seldom to miss the target, the gulli would always obey his command; whether he was looking westwards or eastwards the gulli would invariably reach his hands as if he had it bewitched. Whether it was a new gulli, an old gulli, a small gulli or a big gulli, a pointed gulli or a flat gulli, it would go to him as if his hands were a magnet which attracted them. But today the gulli was indifferent to him and I started tiring him out. I was playing foul, making up for my lack of practice by unfair means. According to the rules of the game, it should have been Gaya's turn. When the gulli was struck hard and fell at some distance, I would run to pick it up. Gaya noticed these irregularities, but he did not raise his voice. Today the gulli was not going straight; instead it was going left or right. After half an hour's exercise, the gulli came in the direction of the danda. It did not hit the danda, it just passed it by. I had played foul, but Gaya did not react.

'It could not hit the danda,' I said, 'for if it had done so, it would have been foul play on my part.'

During my childhood, I could not have won if I played foul. Gaya would have caught me by the neck. But today I am able to cheat him easily. Suddenly, the gulli did hit the danda and hit it so hard as if it were a bullet. And this was warning enough that I had better not play foul.

'But why shouldn't I at least try to make truth look like a falsehood?' I asked myself. 'And why should I lose?' If this were agreed upon, I would win; otherwise I would be tired out. Taking advantage of the approaching darkness, I thought I would be able to get out of this situation…

Gaya then victoriously announced that the gulli had been hit.

Appearing to be unconcerned, I asked, 'Did you see it hit? For I did not.'

'No,' said Gaya. 'It did hit.'

How I said these words at that time is a bit of surprise to me. To turn this falsehood into the truth was like calling the day, night. Both of us saw the gulli hitting the danda. But Gaya did not agree with my statement, 'Yes,' he said, 'the gulli must have hit a brick, because if it had hit the danda the sound produced would have been different.'

I started tiring out Gaya. I felt sorry for his naiveté. Now, when the gulli hit the danda the third time, I decided, large-heartedly, to admit defeat.

'It's now dark, brother,' said Gaya, 'let us meet tomorrow.'

'There will be lots of time tomorrow,' I said, and then thought, 'I don't know how long he will be tiring me out. It would, therefore, be better to sort it out now.'

'No, no,' I said, 'there is still plenty of light, you can take your turn now.'

'But the gulli is hardly visible,' said Gaya.

'Doesn't matter,' I said.

Gaya tried to hit the danda twice. But on both occasions he missed. He finished his turn in two minutes or so. He lost his next turn also in one minute. I now demonstrated my generosity.

'Let us play one more round,' I said. 'You lost the last round.'

'No brother,' he said, 'it is dark now.'

'You seem to be out of practice,' I said. 'Don't you play these days?'

'Where is the time to play?' said Gaya.

We sat in the car, and I drove to the Dak Bungalow before the lamps were lit. Gaya said, 'there will be a game tomorrow. All the old hands will participate. Will you come? If you come, I will invite the others.'

The time for the game was fixed and I went to the field. The players were in groups of ten. Some of them had been my childhood friends but there were also some young men I did not know.

The game started. I watched from my car. I was surprised to see the Gaya's alertness and his expertise. When he hit, the gulli would go high in the sky. The gulli that hit his danda went up 200 yards. None of the hesitation of the previous day was manifest. Had he tired me out the previous day, I would probably have cried.

One young man tired out and played foul. He claimed he had scored. Gaya said the gulli had hit the ground and rebounded. The two challenged each other. When he saw Gaya's flushed face, the youth yielded. There would otherwise have been a fight. Watching their game made me feel the same joy that I experienced in my childhood, when we would lose ourselves in the game ignoring everything else. I realized that Gaya had played the game the previous day hesitantly because he had patronized me. He wasn't really playing. He did not wish to tire me out. My status in life stood between him and me. I can claim respect and generosity from him, but not companionship. In my childhood we were playmates. There was no difference between us. Having risen in life and attained a position, I am now an object of his pity. He now cannot be my equal. He has risen in my eyes, I have fallen…

To go back twenty years when I was at school… The gap between my days at school and government service of several years, was a long one now.

SIX

WHEN I WAS ABOUT THIRTEEN YEARS OLD I WAS QUITE unfamiliar with Hindi, but had a passion for Urdu novels. Maulana Sharar, Pundit Ratan Nath Sarshar, Mirza Ruswa, Maulana Mohammed Ali of Hardoi were the popular novelists of the period. Whenever I came across any of their works, I would forget all about my studies and would not rest until I had read them from cover to cover. In those days Reynolds's novels were in great demand, and their Urdu translations were being published in quick succession. They were my favourites too. The late Hazrat Rias, a well-known poet who had passed away only recently, had translated a novel of Reynolds under the title of *Haram Sara*. The then editor of the Lucknow weekly *Oudh Punch* and one of the immortals among the humourists of India – Maulana Sajjad Hussain – had translated another novel of Reynolds with the title *Tilism-I-Fanus*. I had read all these books. I never grew tired of

Rattan Nath Sarshar even though I had finished reading all his novels.

My father lived in Gorakhpur. I was a student of class VIII or standard III as it was called at the local mission school. There was a bookseller by the name of Buddhilal at Reti. I used to frequent his shop and read novel after novel from his stock. I would take some copies of 'keys' to the English texts and 'notes' and sell them to the students of my school. The bookseller would let me carry home novels that I wished to read. When the stock of novels in the shop was exhausted, I read the Urdu translation of the Puranas, published by the Naval Kishore Press, as well as several parts of *Tilism-i-Hosh-e-Ruba,* a voluminous book of romantic tales. At that time seventeen of these volumes had already been out and each one of them was not less than 200 royal-sized pages long. Besides these seventeen parts, I had read quite a few parts which had been published earlier. It is easy to infer from these books how vast the extent of the author's imagination was. These tales were said to have been written in Persian by Maulana Faizi to entertain Akbar. How far this was true, no one can say. Hardly any work as monumental in any other language exists. It is a veritable encyclopaedia. If anyone were to make a copy of it during his allotted lifespan of three score years, he would not be able to do it. Composing such a work is even less likely.

Around that time, an uncle of mine used to visit us frequently. Though he was well past adolescence he was still unmarried. He owned a small landed estate and a house, but they were of little value to him, and he had no attachment to them. He visited one relative after another and expected everyone to arrange for a match for him. He was always ready to spend Rs 100 or 200. My uncle had a strong physique, long moustache, middling stature and wheatish complexion and it was surprising that he was single. He was addicted to smoking hemp, and his eyes were invariably bloodshot. He was religious in his own way; he offered an oblation of water to Shiva everyday and abstained from eating fish or fowl. However, he did what most unmarried people often do – he fell victim to the arrow of Cupid, shot from the eyes of a chamarin who used to make cow-dung cakes in his house, feed the bullocks and do other odd jobs. She was young and impetuous and, like women of her class, had a smiling face and a playful nature. My uncle's greedy heart stumbled the moment he saw the stream of sweet water. In the midst of conversation, he began to make advances towards her. She gauged his intentions and began to indulge in coquetry. She did her hair with extra oil, even though it was of sesame, brightened her eyes with collyrium and painted her lips. Extra slackness crept into her work. Sometimes she would just peep into the house for a moment and then go away, or cast a glance at him in the evening and then disappear.

The result of all this was that he had to attend to the bullock's feed and other chores himself, for he could ill afford to fall foul of her love. In accordance with custom, he gave her a beautiful, somewhat costly sari of a rich material and also a hefty tip on Holi. Matters went so far that the maidservant became practically the mistress of the house.

One evening the chamars held a meeting of their Panchayat. The members were not afraid of my uncle just because he was more affluent and influential than they were. What they resented was the striking contrast between the behaviour of my uncle's father, who in his lifetime had never looked at a woman lustfully, and his progeny who stared shamelessly at the daughters and wives of the menial class. Persuasion, they felt, would be of no avail. He might, on the contrary, create a serious problem. They thought that they could set the situation right with one stroke. They decided to teach him a lesson he would never forget. Dishonour can be avenged with blood, and punishment can, and does, settle matters to a certain extent.

When Champa, the maidservant, entered the house the following evening, my uncle closed the door of the inner room. The chamars, who had been waiting for such an opportunity, started knocking on the outer door. Uncle thought one of his tenants had come to see him and, finding the door shut, would go back. But when he heard the noise the crowd was making, he was perplexed. He looked out of the keyhole and saw about twenty or twenty-five chamars, all armed with sticks, trying to break open the door. There was no way of escape nor could he hide Champa. He realized that he was now heading for trouble. He had not anticipated that his beloved would precipitate such a crisis or he might have been circumspect in giving his heart away to her. Champa, on her part, was twitting and testing him.

'You will not be a loser in any way,' she said. 'It is I whose honour has been threatened. My people will not leave me alive. I told you with folded hands not to close the door but you were possessed with passion. You have now been well served; you have blackened your own face.'

Poor uncle! He had never traversed this path before. If he had been an expert in the game, he would have hit upon 101 expedients to extricate himself from the predicament. But he was absolutely nonplussed. He stood in the courtyard, reciting the scriptures. Outside the door, the crescendo was rising until the whole village gathered. The Brahmins, the Thakurs, the Kayasths – all had come there to see the excitement and to give a good hiding to the delinquent. What could be more exciting and amusing than to discover a man and a woman shut behind a closed door! However humble or high placed a man might be, the public would never pardon him. A carpenter was sent for. The door was broken open and Uncle was found in the fodder store. Champa was seen standing in the courtyard and crying. As soon as the door opened she fled. No one said a word to her. But he knew there was no reprieve for him. He prepared himself to receive whatever punishment might be meted out to him. Anything anyone could lay his hands on – umbrella, sticks, shoes, fist, leg – were pressed into service to beat him till he swooned and fainted. Thinking he was dead, the crowd left him. Even if he survived, they argued, he would not be able to live any longer in the village; his estate would pass on to somebody else.

The news of this mishap reached us. I enjoyed it immensely. When I tried to picture the features of my uncle as he was being tortured by the villagers, I laughed heartily.

For a month my uncle drank, by way of treatment, a mixture of molasses and turmeric. As soon as he was able to move about, he came to us because he wished to file a suit in our city against his villagers for their criminal assault on him.

If he had shown any repentance or humility I would, perhaps, have sympathized with him. But he was still as arrogant as ever. He threatened to report to my father my fondness for novels and for games. This was to browbeat me, something I could not take from him. I had now a sufficiently strong case against his character.

One day I wove all that had befallen my poor uncle into a play which I read out to my friends. All of them had a hearty laugh. I felt encouraged, made out a fair copy and, keeping it under my uncle's pillow, went to school. I was amused and apprehensive. I was curious to know what my uncle would say after he had read the play. That day, my heart was not in my books but at home. As soon as school was over, I made for home. When I was near it, I stopped short. I feared that Uncle would give me a severe beating. However, I was certain that he would not give me more than one slap because he knew that I was not one of those boys who would take such things lying down.

But my uncle was not on the cot on which he usually stretched out to rest. I wondered if he had gone inside the house. I looked into his room. Silence reigned there and there was no trace of his shoes, clothes or other belongings. I enquired from the other members of the family and learnt that my uncle had, without taking his meals, gone back home on some urgent business. I made a thorough search for my first play – my very first composition – but could not find it anywhere. I do not know if he had consigned it to flames or carried it with him to heaven!

SEVEN

MY FATHER WAS A THOUGHTFUL PERSON WHO WALKED ON the road of life with his eyes wide open. However in his later years he stumbled and in the fall that he sustained, he pushed me down also (got me married). I was barely fifteen then and studying in the ninth class.

I believed that the most beautiful thing in the world is a woman. She symbolizes tenderness and sweetness. At the very mention of the word 'woman' I would be attentive, like a music lover hearing a melody. When I began to think for myself, I used to dream of a beauty who would rule my heart; she would have the glow of dawn, the tenderness of a flower, the light of a diamond, be the very picture of spring and have the sweetness of a cuckoo's voice. Besides, she would have all the qualities portrayed by poets. I was a worshipper of an imaginary beauty. I also spoke to my friends about her and would be lost in thoughts about her.

The day arrived when my hopes and aspirations would bear fruit. My marriage was fixed. I expressed my desire to see the girl of my dreams. But when my uncle assured me that he had himself seen the girl and that she was beautiful, I agreed. The wedding party went with the usual pomp and show. The bride was from Rampur village in Mehndawal tehsil of Basti district. Her father was a zamindar. As per the custom of the eastern region, I was invited inside the house. There were hundreds of women in the house. Everyone was in a merry mood. I felt happy at the fuss being made over me. The women enjoyed teasing me. As I was the only male in the crowd, I felt uncomfortable. However, I was able to get out of the situation.

The auspicious moment of solemnization arrived. The bride, in her finery, was brought into the mandap. I saw her forearm and her feet. How beautiful her fingers were, like the flame of a lamp. She looked attractive. I was happy.

The next day was the bride's farewell. I was restless to get a glimpse of her. On the return journey, en route to my house, the palanquin bearers laid down the palanquin to have a little rest, I quietly slipped to the seat of the bride. She had lifted the veil and was looking out of the palanquin. I saw her. A wave of hatred, anger and helplessness passed through me. She wasn't the great beauty that I had been imagining all these years. She was a flatfaced, flat-nosed, ugly woman with swollen cheeks. Her complexion was fair, but rather than being reddish she was whitish. All my enthusiasm was gone. Was I the only one for her in this wide world? I was angry with the uncle who had praised her looks. Had he been around I would have given him a thrashing.

Life was now hell for me. I ran down the uncle, ticked off the father-in-law and revolted against my parents. When all this did not work, I thought of running away from home. At times I felt sorry for my wife too. What's her fault, I asked myself, she did not force herself on me. However, pity and compassion could not subdue the feeling of hatred which I had for her. She dressed well; did her hair and would sit before the mirror to make herself attractive. She tried her best to please me. She searched for occasions to lure me. But I avoided her or kept a safe distance from her. If there was a face-to-face encounter, I would rebuke her so that she would start crying and leave me alone.

I tried to forget that I was a married man. For days on end she wouldn't see me, although she heard guffaws of laughter from me and my friends. She would peep through a hole to see me going around with my arms around my friends.

One day, while dining together, she said to me, 'These days I don't even see you. Would you leave home because of me…?'

'No,' I said. 'I am always around. I am in search of a job these days.'

Then my wife said, 'I hear there are cosmetic doctors. Why don't you ask the doctor to give me a face lift?'

'Why do you provoke me?' I asked her. 'Who asked you to come to me?'

'Who can cure me of my malady?' she asked me.

'There is no remedy,' I said. 'What God could not do, how can a man?'

She said, 'It is for you to see. Why should you punish me for God's fault?'

'Is there anyone in this world,' she asked, 'who does not like a pretty face. But have you ever come across an ugly man who remains unmarried? Even ugly girls don't stay forever at their parent's houses. Somehow or the other they all get married. The husband may not be ready to sacrifice everything for such a wife, but the husband certainly does not discard her like a fly in milk.'

Somewhat irritated, I said to her, 'I am not getting into a confrontation with you. One's heart cannot be controlled at will.

Nor can it be influenced by logic and argument. I haven't said anything to hurt you. Why then are you entering into an argument with me?'

She heard all this and left in a huff, because she knew that her husband's heart was in the right place.

I didn't return home every day. The wife suffered and became sickly. Yet I stayed away. Sometimes I wished she would die so that I would be liberated from her. The next time I would marry someone really nice.

When I was born, my father earned about Rs 20 a month. Before he reached the stage of Rs 40 he was dead. The family income was little, and all the savings had been spent either on my father's six-month illness or on his last rites. It was for me to earn and support not only my wife, but also my stepmother and her two children.

It was as difficult then to get a job as it is now. With very great effort I could perhaps have found a job for Rs 10 to Rs 12 a month. But I had the ambition of getting an M.A. degree and becoming a lawyer. While my feet were thus bound with chains wrought not just of iron but of the heaviest-known metal, I wanted to climb the Everest!

There was inflation. Barley was being sold at ten seers for a rupee! My feet were bare. My clothes were in tatters. Thanks to the headmaster of Queen's College, Banaras, I had a freeship. My examination was ahead of me. I would leave my village for school before 8.00 a.m., seldom reach there on time, and leave school at 3.30 p.m. to walk to Bans ka Phatak to coach a boy. When I would be free at 6.00 p.m., I would walk five miles back to the village, seldom reaching home before 8.00 p.m., no matter how fast I walked. I would dine, sit down and fall asleep. Despite all these tribulations, however, I did not lose heart, and somehow passed the matriculation examination, securing only a second division. As the freeship was possible only for those who had a first division, admission to Queen's College was out of my reach.

A Hindu college had, however, been started that very year. Seeing a possibility of being admitted to it, I went to the house of Mr Richardson, the Principal. Dressed in a dhoti and kurta he squatted on the floor in the Indian fashion and was engaged in writing. It was easy to have taken to Indian clothes; but the adoption of the Indian manner was not so easy. After listening to a part of my request – I had said only a few of the words I had wanted to say – he told me bluntly that he did not discuss matters pertaining to the college at home and that, therefore, I should see him at the college the next day. The following day, I went to the college. My meeting with him was disheartening. I was told that I could not get a freeship. If I could bring some eminent person's influence to bear upon the college authorities, I knew that my request for a freeship would be granted. But who was there in this town who would recommend the case of a rustic lad? To whom could I tell my tale of woe? There was none who could do anything for me. I persisted in my attempts nevertheless. To leave my house, trek about twelve miles and return home disappointed became my daily routine.

One day I met Thakur Indra Narain Singh, a member of the managing committee of the college and told him of my plight. He sympathized with me and gave me a letter of recommendation. My happiness at that moment was unbounded. I returned home elated, determined to meet the Principal again on the following day.

As soon as I reached home, however, I got a fever. For a full fortnight I was confined to bed. I drank concoctions of neem – to the point of disgust. The fever, however, continued. One day, while I sat at the doorstep, the village priest was passing by. He saw me and enquired about my welfare. When I told him of my sad predicament, he went into the fields and brought a herb, along with a few corns of black pepper, ground them and administered the mixture to me. The medicine wrought a miracle.

When I met the college Principal after a month and showed him the recommendatory letter, he fixed his gaze on me and asked me where I had been all these days.

'I was sick,' I said.

'What was the ailment?'

I was not prepared for this question. Fever, according to my understanding, was a mild ailment and could not justify absence for a long time. If, therefore, I said that I had fever, the Principal might think that I was telling a lie. I should, thus, mention some ailment, the affliction of which would arouse his pity. I could not think of any ailment on the spur of the moment other one – palpitation of the heart – which Thakur Indra Narain Singh had mentioned to me when I had gone to see him.

'Palpitation of the heart, Sir,' I said to the Principal. He was taken aback. He looked at me intently and asked me: 'Are you all right now?'

'Yes, Sir.'

'Fill in the application form for admission.'

I brought the form, filled it in and presented it to the Principal who was then taking a class. At 3 p.m., I got it back, with his remarks: 'To be put to test for his ability.'

Only those who do not secure admission elsewhere go to newly opened institutions which are like a hungry man who eats up everything he gets initially but becomes choosy after having a full meal.

I had no hope of successfully passing in the test in any subject other than English language. The thought of arithmetic and geometry frightened me; I had forgotten the little I knew of these subjects.

But there was no way out. Putting my faith in luck, therefore, I went into the classroom, presented the form, and sat in the last row. The teacher, a Bengali, was teaching English lessons – the story of Rip Van Winkle. He impressed me. After the period was over, he asked me several questions on the day's lesson and put 'satisfactory' on my application form.

The next test was that of arithmetic. I presented my application to the teacher, again a Bengali. He put my arithmetic to test; I failed. He, therefore, wrote 'unsatisfactory' on my application form. I was now so downcast that I did not go to the Principal again, and returned home instead – arithmetic to me was like climbing the peak of the Kailash mountain; I could never climb it, I had failed twice in my intermediate because of weak arithmetic, gave up the attempt, and succeeded in passing the examination after ten or twelve years, i.e., when arithmetic was no longer a compulsory subject and one could offer another optional subject instead.

I returned home a disappointed man. Sitting at home I could do nothing to achieve the immediate goal of admission to college. For this I felt that I must improve my arithmetic, which held the key to my admission into a college. It appeared necessary, therefore, to live in the town.

As good luck would have it, a class fellow of mine got me the assignment of a private coach to the son of his lawyer brother-in-law in Banaras. I got Rs 5 a month, lived on two and sent the rest home. I sought the lawyer's permission to live in the decrepit room above his stable, bought a little kerosene oil lamp and sat on a gunny bag that I spread on the floor. In the utensils I had brought from my home, I would cook khichri once a day, eat it, clean the dishes and go to the library to study arithmetic. But the study of arithmetic was only an excuse and a ruse to read novels – *Fasana-i-Azad, Chandrakanta Santati* and as many Urdu translations of Bankim Chandra Chatterjee as there were in the library.

The friendship of the class fellow who got me this assignment helped me borrow money whenever I needed to. Of course I would clear the accounts as soon as I got my wages. At times I was left with only Rs 2 or, at the most, with Rs 3. Even this account was enough to make me lose my equanimity. The temptation for sweets would overpower me and lead me to the sweetmeat shop where I would gorge sweets worth two to three annas. It was only after I had done this, that I would visit my home in the village and give my people the remaining Rs 2–3. However, there were occasions when I would feel shy of borrowing money and spend days without food. Once, I took a piece of cloth worth about Rs 2 on credit from a draper who saw me pass by his shop everyday and who trusted me. When I could not pay him for a month or two, I felt so ashamed of myself that I stopped going that way and took a detour. It took me three years to pay him his dues.

It was again around this period that I borrowed a half rupee from a workman in Banaras. He had come to take Hindi lessons from me, and lived at the back of the lawyer's house. ('Know this, my brother' was his affectation and we called him 'Know-this-my-brother'.) He came to my village five years later to realize this amount from me. These are some of my tribulations and frustrations.

Despite my keenness to get a higher education, I was forced to look for a job. But I did not know how to get one.

I starved for two days. I was hungry and did not have a single paisa. My shopkeeper refused to lend me anything more (or maybe I was hesitant to borrow anything).

The winter evening approached fast and it was lighting time. Disappointed everywhere, I decided to sell the 'key' to Chakravarti's book on arithmetic, which I had bought two years earlier. I went to a book seller and sold it for a rupee, that is exactly half its price.

As I was stepping down from the shop, a well-built moustached man who sat at the shop asked me where I studied.

'I am no longer studying,' I said, 'but hope to get admission into some college.'

'Are you a matriculate?' he asked me.

'Yes, I am.'

'Don't you want a job?'

'I do. But I cannot get one.'

My questioner was the headmaster of a small school. He wanted an assistant teacher and offered Rs 18 a month. I accepted his offer. The sum of Rs 18 was very much beyond my frustration-eroded imagination and when I left him with a promise to meet him the next day, I could not walk straight. This was in 1899.

EIGHT

THE PRIMARY SCHOOL WHERE I GOT THE JOB WAS ABOUT eleven miles from my home. The headmaster of this school was obsessed with teaching. The boys would have their dinner and then come to the school where he would lie on a cot and snore loudly. Whenever there was some loud talk or noise he would suddenly wake up from his slumber, give a few slaps to the children and then return to his land of dreams. This happened everyday till midnight. Some of the children would also fall asleep on the jute mattress.

The annual examination was due in April, but hectic preparations would start in January. In the night school, the children were spared this trouble, but there were never any holidays. Somawati Amavasya, Basant and Shiv Ratri came and went, but no holidays. There was no need to mention Sundays. To go out and travel even for a day, according to the headmaster, was meaningless. As a result, I had not been able to visit my family home for several months. On the occasion of Holi I decided that I would go home, even if this meant quitting my job. I gave the headmaster an advance ultimatum that as Holi would fall on 20 March, I would leave for home on the evening of 19 March. The headmaster sahib told me that I was young and did not know how difficult it was to get a job these days. In fact, he said, getting a job was not half as difficult as the ability to keep one. 'Examinations are scheduled for April,' he said. 'Imagine how many children would pass if the school remained closed for three or four days. Would not the labour put in over the whole year be wasted? So you do as I tell you. Don't go home during these holidays; instead, go during the holidays falling after the examinations are over. And there would then be four holidays on the occasion of Easter. I won't ask you then to forego even one day's leave.'

But I stuck to my resolve. Neither persuasion nor threats of show cause notice had any effect on me.

After school was over on 19 March, I came to my house quietly and left without even saying goodbye to the headmaster. If I had gone to say goodbye to him, he would have asked me to stay on for one assignment or another, e.g., totalling the fees in the register, or calculating the average attendance or collecting the boys' answer books, arranging them datewise, etc.

Back at my house, I hurriedly picked up a bundle of books and a bedroll, put them on my shoulders and left for the railway station. The train was due to leave at 17.05 hours. The school had closed at 16.00 hours. I had thought there would be enough time to reach the railway station. But the school clock was misleading; as it turned out, it was half an hour slow. Like all railway passengers wishing to reach the railway station before the train, I walked as fast as I could.

The bundle of books on my shoulders was heavy; so was the bedroll. I in turn changed their sides and ran faster.

The railway station was visible from a distance of two furlongs. The signal, I saw, was down. So was my courage. I ran for about 100 steps, feeling despair. I saw from a distance the railway train arriving, halting for a minute and then departing.

It was now meaningless to reach the station. The next train was scheduled to leave at 11 p.m. and I would thus reach the station closest to my home past midnight. And it would take me another hour to reach home. To walk in the stillness of night would have been an adventure for which I was unprepared. I even thought of returning to school and ticking off the headmaster for the trick played by the school clock. But I restrained myself and decided to walk the entire distance. It was only twelve miles or so. Walking at two miles an hour, it would take me six hours and if I walked fast, I could perhaps reach home by 10 o'clock. Mother and Mannu would be waiting for me. And as soon as I reached home, I would get a hot meal. Close by was a place where sugarcane juice was made into gur. They would get me warm juice too. And wouldn't the neighbours be surprised that I had walked all the way.

I headed for the banks of the river Ganga. I stood at a point close to the river bank; my village was across the river, I had never walked on this road but I had heard that the kachcha pathway led in that direction. In any case, there was nothing to worry about, I thought. The boat would transport me across the river in ten minutes and then I'd start walking. The distance to be covered was only twelve miles or six kos.

When I reached the ghat on the river bank, I saw that the boat was not even half full. I jumped into it and sat down. I even took out the fare to be paid to the boatman. But the boatman would not sail until it was full. People who have to report to the tehsil office or the district courts come one by one, and then sit down gingerly in the boat. But I felt restless, because I saw that the sun was racing down as if it was competing with my thought process. It was white but fast turning yellow. In no time it would turn red. It hung across the river like a bucket perched on a wall. There was a nip in the air too. I felt hungry. In my enthusiasm to reach home and the turmoil before my departure, I had not made chapattis. I had thought I would reach home in time for a meal. Also, I had thought, parched gram worth a paisa would be enough for me. But all this did not come about. In any case, I also thought, there would be some shops where I could buy some sweets for four paisa or so.

By the time the boat transported me across the river, it was nearing the sun's last gasp and the bottom of the boat was almost touching the bed of the river. I picked up the bundle that I had and started walking. On both sides of the pathway were fields in which the crimson coloured flowers of the gram crop had a thin film of dew. I entered one field, pulled out gram plants and ran. Ahead of me was a distance of twelve miles. It was a kachcha pathway through an uninhabited tract.

The sun had now set. I now realized that I had made a mistake. The enthusiasm of my youth said, 'No problem at all. I can run for one or two miles.' I multiplied the twelve miles by the yard per mile and calculated that it would be just 20,000 yards. The 20,000 yards sounded easier than twelve miles. When it would be about three miles before my village, I would be almost there; these two or three miles would not matter. I saw some passengers follow me. This gave me hope.

It was now dark. From a distance I saw a cottage on the roadside. And there was a light in the cottage. 'It must be a bania's shop,' I said to myself. 'It would certainly have something to eat, at least some gur and parched gram. Let me walk fast.'

I reached there and stopped opposite the cottage. Four or five people were sitting there and they had bottles in front of them. A short distance away there was someone roasting peas. Its sweet smell was like an electric current passing through my body. Somewhat restless, I put my hand in the pocket to take out a paisa. I advanced towards the people and then stopped opposite a liquor shop.

'What do you want?' asked the vendor. To him liquor was the most important thing. The people sitting there, I thought, would either be washermen or chamars. Who else in the village would drink liquor? But the strong smell of roasted peas attracted me and I advanced forward.

The bundle of my bedroll was irksome. I felt like throwing it away on the road. It must have been about ten pounds in weight but it seemed like a maund. In any case, I felt weak.

The moon of the fifteenth night seemed perched on the tree, peeping at the earth below through the leaves. Though I walked, I did not feel any ache or pain. These were perhaps redundant. Or perhaps my hunger was the dominant feeling that had made the pain less potent.

Then I smelt gur. It must be being made somewhere close by, I said to myself. Perhaps there is also a village nearby. I saw a light peeping through the mango grove. But would there be someone who would sell me gur worth a paisa or two. I would not be able to ask the gur maker to give me gur for this meagre amount. I didn't know what the people would make of my request, but I advanced. I love gur so much that whenever I have thought of opening a shop, I have thought it would sell sweetmeats. Whether or not the shop would be able to sell sweets, there would be sweets for me to eat anyway. Look at the sweetmeat sellers. They are so fat that they cannot move easily.

But then they are foolish, I though, because they live a life of extreme ease. That's why they develop paunches. When I start a sweetmeat shop, I thought prudently, I would continue to exercise.

The smell of gur was trying my patience and whetting my appetite. I recall the time when my mother went to her parents' house, and I polished off a maund of gur.

However, I must admit that the sweet smell of gur made me completely oblivious of all other things. Exercising self-restraint, I moved on. My body was under such strain that my legs were trembling. The kachcha pathway had grooves made in it by the bullock-cart wheels. When my feet were caught in these grooves, I felt as if I had sunk into a pit.

Several times I felt like lying on the roadside. The weight of the bundle of books felt as if it were about one maund. I cursed myself for bringing these books along. I had thought of sitting for an examination in another language, but there was no occasion for even opening these books during the holidays. I brought along this weight unnecessarily really. In fact, I felt so irritated that I thought of throwing away the books. I felt my legs refuse to walk. I fell down twice. When I got up, I saw my legs were trembling. It seemed impossible to go ahead on an empty stomach. And there was nothing that I could get to eat. I felt like weeping.

Then I saw a field of sugarcane. I could not resist the temptation to take out three or four canes and chew them while I continued to walk. I thought it would help me to walk and also fill my stomach with sugar juice. However, when I put my foot on the divider it got entangled in a thorny bush. The owner of the field had possibly spread this barbed bush on the boundary. My shirt and my dhoti were caught in it. When I retraced my steps, the thorny bush was dragged along. As I tried to disentangle my clothes, the barbs injured my hands. When I tried further to pull it with some force, my dhoti was torn. While I was lost in this new struggle, my hunger was forgotten. If I got rid of the thorns on one side, they would get stuck on the other side. If I bent, they would pierce my body. If I were to shout, my attempt to thieve would be exposed. I was indeed in deep trouble. I wept at my sad plight. I don't think even any lover wandering in desolate deserts would have had such trouble from thorns.

After half an hour of struggle, I was, with great difficulty, able to extricate myself from this situation. My dhoti and kurta had been torn, my hands and my feet were like sieves. It was torturous to go forward even one step and I did not know how much distance I had covered and how much remained. There was no one I could ask in sight.

Then I saw a village in the distance. I was overjoyed because I thought there would certainly be a shop where I could eat and lie down in a covered verandah till the next morning. But people in the villages are accustomed to go to bed early. I saw one man drawing water from a well. When I asked him for information he was curt.

'You won't get anything to eat here,' he said. 'The shopkeeper keeps only the bare necessities, and there is no shop selling sweets. This is not a city. And who would keep shops open at night.'

Entreating him, I said, 'Will there be a place where I can sleep?'

He asked me who I was and whether there was anyone in the village who knew me.

'Well, if someone here knew me,' I said, 'why should I be asking you?'

'Well, my friend,' he said, 'none in this village will allow a stranger to stay here. Yesterday a traveller came and stayed here, and there was a theft in a house here that night. And the traveller was not seen the next morning.'

'Am I a thief?' I asked.

'No,' he said, 'but a thief does not write that he is one across his face.'

'Well, you may not allow me to stay here for the night, but please don't call me a thief. Had I known that this village is so horrible, I would not have come here.'

I did not pursue the matter with him any further because I was hurt. I returned to the road and started walking again. I was not in my senses and had lost my bearings. I did not know the road by which I had entered the village or in which direction I was proceeding. I had no hope of reaching my destination. I realized that the night would pass as I continued to loiter about like this. I don't really know for how long I was in this state.

Then, suddenly, I saw a fire lit in the field. I thought I might find a place to pass the night there. I walked fast. When I was approaching the field, a huge dog barked loudly. His bark was so loud that I shivered in fear. Soon, it was facing me and barking furiously. In my hands, I had nothing except the bundle of books. I had no stick, no stone. If it pounced on me or pulled my leg, what would I do? It appeared to be a dog of foreign breed. As I tried to shut it up, its bark became louder. Then, putting aside the bundle of books on the roadside, I stood still and took off my shoe, so that I had something to protect myself with. I was looking at the dog intently. Should he advance towards me and come too close to me, I would hit him with the heel of my shoe and with such force that he would remember it always. Perhaps the dog read my thoughts. He pounced on me with such force that I shivered and my shoe fell down on the ground. I then shouted, 'Is there anyone in this field? Please come and save me from this dog...oh Mahato, the dog is about to bite me.'

I heard someone reply – 'Who is it?'

'I am a traveller,' I said. 'Your dog is biting me.'

'No, he won't bite you, don't be afraid. And where do you have to go?'

'To Mahmoodnagar,' I said.

'You have left behind the road to Mahmoodnagar. It is certainly not ahead of you.'

I was crestfallen. 'How far back is the road to Mahmoodnagar?' I asked him, disappointed.

'Just about three miles,' he said.

A giant of a man appeared, holding a lantern in his hand. He had on a hat, an army overcoat, a pair of shorts and full boots. He was tall and hefty, had a big moustache and fair complexion. A very handsome man indeed.

'You appear to be a student from some school,' he said.

'No,' I said, 'I am not a student. I teach students, and am going home. I have three days off.'

'Why didn't you go by train?' he asked.

'The train had departed and the next train was at an hour past midnight.'

'You can board it now. It is around twelve. Come, I shall show you the way to the railway station.'

'Which station is it?' I asked.

'Bhagwantpur,' he said.

'But I started from Bhagwantpur. It must be quite a few miles back.'

'No, you are just under one mile from Bhagwantpur. Come I'll show you the way to the Bhagwantpur railway station. You'll be able to board the train there. However, if you wish you can stay the night in my cottage and leave tomorrow morning.'

I was angry with myself. I had been at it since 5 o'clock and I was just one mile from Bhagwantpur. I had lost my way. I shall always remember this event and also that I had walked for six hours and covered just one mile. The desire to reach home now asserted itself. 'No,' I said, 'tomorrow is Holi and I must reach home tonight.'

'The pathway is rocky,' he said. 'You may have to face wild beasts too. Anyway, come, I'll take you to the railway station. But let me tell you that you have made a great mistake. It is dangerous to travel on a road you do not know. But wait here, I will come.' The dog wagged his tail and appeared keen to befriend me. His head was bent low as if wanting to be forgiven, and he wagged his tail and stood before me.

Large-heartedly, I forgave him and put my hand on his head.

In a short while, the man appeared with a gun on his shoulder and said, 'Come now, but don't commit such a mistake again. It is your good luck that you met me. Had you reached the river bank, you surely would have encountered wild beasts.'

'You appear to be an Englishman,' I said, 'but you speak our language fluently.'

He laughed and said. 'Yes, my father was an Englishman...He was an officer in the army. My mother served him as a cook. I live here. I too have served in the army and fought in the war in Europe, and now draw a pension. The scenes of war that I saw with my own eyes and the manner in which I had to live and kill people made me disgusted with the profession. That's why I opted for a pension and came here. My father had built a small house here. I live in that house and guard the fields around. We are in the Ganga valley. All around are hills. Wild beasts roam here; boars, neelgai and deer. They destroy crops. My job is to protect the crops from their ravages. I get one maund of foodgrains from each farmer. That's enough for my upkeep. My old mother is still around. She cooks for me as she cooked for my father. Come over sometime. I'll teach you physical exercises. You will become a wrestler in a year's time.'

'Do you still exercise?' I asked.

'Yes, I exercise for two hours everyday. I am very fond of wielding the club. I do gymnastics. I am now in my fiftieth year and yet I can run for five miles at a stretch. How can I exist in this wilderness without exercise? I had wrestling bouts. I was the strong man of my regiment. However, when I think of the life of an armyman I feel sorry and remorseful and my head bows in shame. Many innocent men died through my wielding the rifle. What harm had they done to me? What enmity existed between them and me? I thought that the German and Austrian soldiers were as brave, truthful, happy and sympathetic as the French and the British. We had become friends, we played together, we sat together. We never felt that they were not our comrades. And yet we hungered for the blood of each other and this was so because the big merchants of England were afraid lest the Germans take away their businesses. This is rule by the merchants. Our armies are mere pawns in their hands. The poor lost their lives and the rich lined their pockets. We were looked after very well; we were patted on the back. We were showered with fruits; we were entertained at garden parties, and our bravery on the battlefield was publicized through illustrations in daily newspapers. Fair ladies and princesses stitched clothes for us. And they also prepared all sorts of delicacies for us. After the peace treaty was signed, nobody bothered about us in the least. Many lost their limbs and became lame or blind. There was no one to give them even a loaf of bread. I have seen many of them begging on the roadside. Ever since the war I have hated this profession. I came here to take up this work and I am happy I did so. It is soldiery all right, but it ensures the protection of the lives and property of the poor, and doesn't make millionaires richer. My life here is in danger...I have escaped death several times. However, this work is such that even if I lay down my life, I won't feel sorry, because I would be happy that my life has been of service to the poor. And

I cannot really tell you about the love and care which the poor people shower on me. If I fall sick and they think that their blood would help me recover, they would donate it gladly. My father had left me enough resources. If I knew how to live frugally, I could have lived a life of ease. But drinking played havoc with my system. I used to live in great style, with collars and ties – a dandy. I used to flirt with beautiful girls and women. I gambled in horse races and drank heavily, played cards in the club and spent time with ladies. Such then was my life. In three or four years, I wasted Rs 25,000. Nothing was left even for my last rites. When I finished all the money, I thought of taking up a job. That is how I joined the army. Thank God, I left the army after having learnt a lot. It became clear to me that the brave don't put an end to life, they protect it.

'On my return from Europe, I took to shikaar. One day I came here. I saw many farmers standing downcast at the edge of the fields. I asked them what the matter was. One of them said, "Neither death comes to us, nor good crops. Wild animals come and destroy our crops. How then do we pay the taxes or the dues of the mahajan and how do we pay the zamindar's agents? Not very long ago, the plentiful crops here were a sight to see. But today they are all destroyed. Wild animals have eaten all that there was."

'I heard all this, and I don't know which God or prophet gave me inspiration. I took pity on them. From that day onwards, I told them that I would protect their crops. I'd see that no beast damages them. If they damage the crops I would pay a fine. And from that day to this day, this is what I have done. I have not shirked the self-imposed duty even for a day. It is now ten years since that day. I earn my livelihood and earn the gratitude of the people. And I feel happy.'

We reached the river bank. I saw that this was the ghat where I had sat in the boat. In the moonlight, the river looked bedecked.

'What's your name?' I asked. 'I will certainly come and see you some time.'

He raised the lantern and focussed light on my face. 'My name is Jackson,' he said. 'Bill Jackson. You must come by sometime. If you ask anyone near the railway station, they will give you my address.' He then turned back and said to me. 'You may have to spend the whole night here. Your mother would be worried. Sit on my shoulders, and I'll take you to the other side of the river. The river is shallow these days and I often swim.'

Full of gratitude, I said to him, 'Isn't what you have done for me more than enough? Otherwise, it would not have been possible for me to reach this place. I'll sit here and cross the river by boat in the morning.'

'But your mother would be worrying no end, wondering what has happened to her dear son.' Saying this, Jackson lifted me on to his shoulders, and, without any fear, got into the water as if it were a dry bed. I held his head in my two arms. But my heart was pounding fast and there was a vibration in my veins. Jackson, however, waded through the water coolly. The water was knee deep. Then it came up to the navel and then as high as his heart. Every step forward was now heavy and I was really afraid. Water now touched his neck and licked my feet. I felt like telling him, 'For God's sake, let us go back. But I could not say these words. To meet the situation, every entrance of my consciousness had been shut. I was afraid that if Jackson slipped that would have been the end of me; he was a swimmer and would be able to cross the river but I would be food for the waves. I felt sorry for not having learnt swimming. All of a sudden, Jackson lifted me in his hands above his shoulders. We were in midstream. The current was so strong that each step took a minute. I had waded through the river in daytime but now at night and in midstream it seemed as if I was facing death. I was literally hanging by Jackson's hands. Then the water receded. I did not see it, but I think that the water had swept over Jackson's head. That's why he must have lifted me in his hands. When his head was above water, he said with great laughter, 'Well, at last you have reached.'

'You had to undergo a lot of trouble for my sake,' I said.

Jackson now put me down, back on his shoulders and said. 'I've never had such pleasure as I did today, not even when I killed the German captain. Tell your mother to pray for me.'

On reaching the ghat, I took leave of Jackson with an unforgettable imprint of his goodness, selfless service and unusual courage on my mind...I wished I could be of some service to the people.

When I reached home at 3 o'clock, the Holi fire had been lit. I ran two miles from the railway station to my home. I don't know how my body, without food, was able to make it.

Hearing my voice, mother came out into the courtyard and hugged me.

'Where have you been all night?' she asked. 'I have been waiting for you since the evening. Come now and eat something. Have you eaten anything?'

My mother is now in the other world. But her loving face is still before my mind's eye and her endearing voice echoes in my ears.

I have met Jackson several times since. The nobility of his character had made me his bhakta. He is not a human being; he is an angel.

***

Shortly thereafter I took up a job in a government primary school in Bahraich. From Bahraich I was transferred to Partapgarh, then Allahabad and later to Kanpur. This was in 1905.

NINE

MY WIFE WAS AN UNFORTUNATE WOMAN, NOT AT ALL good-looking and, although I was not satisfied with her, I pulled along uncomplainingly, like all traditional husbands.

She and my stepmother did not get on well. During the summer holidays, I had just passed one fortnight when domestic differences erupted. The two women hurled invectives at each other.

My wife, in desperation, attempted suicide by hanging with a rope. At midnight my mother got scent of it, rushed and unfastened the rope. I came to know of what had happened only on the following morning. I lost my temper and felt desperate at what she had tried to do. My wife was now adamant that she wouldn't stay with me any longer and would go to her parents' home. I did not have any money. So I raised some money against the revenue of land owned by us and made arrangements for her departure. I did not accompany her.

For a week, there was no letter and no message. I was quite unhappy with her. No, I hated her very sight. The separation this time, I hoped, would be eternal. I prayed I'd live without a wife. For, if the cat is merciful, the poultry can certainly survive without feathers.

My maternal grandfather's family was keen that I remarry. When I told them that I was penniless and did not have enough to live on, my mother said to me that what was required of me was only my consent and that I wouldn't have to spend even a penny. The proposed bride, I was told, was pretty, well brought up and without any expenditure. However, I needed to consult with friends. After due deliberation, I decided to marry a child widow. She was fearless, bold, uncompromising, sincere, amenable to a fault and awfully impulsive. You could not bend her, otherwise she might have broken. I am happy with her, not claiming what she cannot give me. She has picked up some literary tastes and sometimes writes short stories.

My own literary life started in 1901 when my first article was published. I wrote on different subjects for Urdu weeklies and monthlies. I also wrote life sketches of great men of the past and present. I entered government service and continued writing during my leisure hours. I had an insatiable hunger for novels and read whatever I could lay my own hands on, irrespective of their worth.

I started writing my first* novel in 1901. It was *Hum Khurma-O-Hum Savab*. Then came *Kishna*. These are my early works. The former was published by Naval Kishore Press of Lucknow and the latter by Medical Hall, Banaras. These works have all the marks of immaturity. I got my first Hindi novel *Prema* published by the

Indian Press of Allahabad. Apart from satisfying my ego, these books brought me nothing. Writing was only a hobby to me and I could not have dreamt that one day I would become an author.

Before 1907, I did not write a single short story. I got the inspiration to write stories after reading Rabindranath Tagore's short stories. I read them in English, translated some of them into Urdu and got them published in periodicals. Ratan Nath Sarshar, Rabindranath Tagore, Tolstoy and Romain Rolland influenced me but I have evolved my own style.

My first short story, *Duniya ka Anmol Rattan,* was published in 1907. I was writing under the pen name of Navab Rai. I followed this up with another four or five stories. These stories were written with the premise that the literature of a nation reflects the march of time. The ideas which move it and the emotions that are echoed in the hearts of the people are reflected in its prose and verse, like one's image in a mirror. Literature in the earlier phase of our national life, when the people were steeped in ignorance, consisted of nothing except a few love songs or a few degenerate short stories. The second phase began when a life-and-death struggle took place between the old ideas and new ideas and attention came to be devoted to the plans for bringing about reform in the social system.

The stories of this phase revolved round the theme of social reform. The partition of Bengal had awakened ideas of revolt in the hearts of the people. Those ideas could not fail to influence literature. The short stories during this time reflected the beginning of this influence. As ideas crystallized, literature of this type became increasingly popular. A collection of stories was published under the title *Soz-I-Vatan* by the Zamana Press.

I was then a deputy inspector of schools in the Education Department and was posted in Hamirpur district, U.P. Within six months of the publication of the book, I received urgent summons from the Collector, then on tour, asking me to see him at once. It was a wintry night. I got the bullock-cart ready and started immediately. After travelling thirty to forty miles, I reached the Collector's camp. When I saw him, I found that he had a copy of my *Soz-I-Vatan* before him. I felt uneasy, because I had already got scent that the Intelligence Department was in search of the book's author. Obviously they had succeeded in tracking him.

'Are you the author of this book?' asked the Collector.

'Yes,' I said.

He asked me the gist of each story and, when I had finished, he flared up. 'These stories of yours are full of sedition,' he said. 'You should thank your stars that you are a British subject. Had it been the time of the Moghuls, your hands would have been cut off. You have insulted the British government.'

I was asked to hand over all the copies of the book to the government, and to never write again without the government's prior permission. Of the 1,000 copies printed, only 300 had been sold. I got the remaining 700 from the Zamana office and presented them to the Collector. I thought the storm was over, and that I had got off cheaply, but authority was not to be appeased so easily. The Collector subsequently conferred with his two deputies – the Superintendent of Police and the Deputy Inspector of Schools under whom I served – to decide my fate. One of the Deputy Collectors, I learnt, quoted extracts from my stories to prove that, from beginning to end, there was nothing in them but sedition. According to the police, such a dangerous man should be punished.

The other, the Deputy Inspector who was fond of me, wished to prevent the matter from taking an awkward turn. He suggested that, if desired, he could, in a friendly way, ascertain my political views and submit a report. He had thought that he would caution me and submit a report saying that the exclusive interest of the author of the book was writing, and that he was not connected with any political agitation.

The committee accepted this suggestion, shelving the proposals made by the police.

'Do you think that he would tell you of his innermost thoughts?' the Collector asked the Deputy Inspector.

'Yes, I know him fairly well.'

'You want to become his friend to find out his secrets,' said the Collector. 'This, I think, amounts to spying, and I consider it mean.'

'It is only to obey your orders...' stuttered the Deputy Inspector.

'These are not my orders,' interrupted the Collector. 'I don't want to give such an order. If the charge of sedition is proved, he should be tried in an open court. Otherwise, he should be let off with a warning. I hate hypocrisy.'

When all this was told to me by the Deputy Inspector several days later, I asked him, 'Would you have really spied on me?'

He laughed. 'Impossible,' he said. 'I would not do it, even if someone had offered me Rs 1,00,000. I only wanted to stop the case from going to a court of law; for, if the case had gone to a court, nobody would have pleaded your cause and a sentence was a certainty. I succeeded in my efforts. The Collector, you will agree, is kind.'

'Very kind, indeed,' I said.

* * *

When my department threatened me with action and told me not to write without prior permission, on the advice of friend Daya Narain Nigam, I, bade goodbye to my pen name Navab Rai and adopted the pen name Premchand.

While travelling in areas around Hamirpur, I found that it was not possible to get fresh vegetables during the summer months. For days on end, therefore, all that I could eat was dried arvi which survives like a scorpion. Its harmful effect, I thought, could be countered by ajvain. I, therefore, took the two together. It had no adverse effect for ten or twelve days. In fact, my appetite improved, possibly due to the climate of the Bundhelkhand mountains. But a few days later, I had a stomach ache. It was so acute that I writhed like a fish out of water. I tried every treatment possible in the village – hot water bottle, phakki and jamun arak. But the pain continued. The following day I got an attack of dysentery. There was mucus in the stool. The pain disappeared.

A month later, the police inspector of a town I was visiting invited me to stay with him. Fed up with the daily fare of pulses, I accepted his invitation in the fond hope that I would get some delicious food for a change. The police inspector served zimin qand, pulao and dahi bade. I ate only two mouthfuls of zimin qand but within two hours of my going into the police inspector's thatched hut I was in pain. I squirmed the whole night and the following day I drank soda water, vomited and felt a little relief. I thought this was all due to zimin quand. I had already given up arvi, now I was giving up zimin qand also. The very sight of these two vegetables makes me nervous.

The pain left me, but dysentery made my body its abode. There was also ceaseless distension and wind. Regular walks of four to five miles, regulated hours of eating, exercise, and some medicine or the other did not improve the situation. The dysentery continued and my body disintegrated. I visited Kanpur for treatment several times, and once I got Yunani and allopathic treatment for a whole month at Allahabad. But all this was in vain.

Then I asked for a transfer. While I wanted Rohilkhand, I was sent to Basti in the Terai area. It was my good fortune, however, that there I came into contact with Mannan Dwivedi Gajpuri, the Tehsildar of Domariaganj, with whom I would discuss literature.

My dysentery was aggravated. I took six months' leave and went to the medical college at Lucknow. Disappointed there, I tried Yunani medicines at Banaras. After three or four months I did feel a little better but the ailment was not eradicated. When, therefore, I returned to Basti, the symptoms persisted. I left the touring job and got myself posted as a teacher in the High School at Basti. I derived inspiration from Dwivedi to get back to novel-writing. Thus began *Sevasadan**.

From Basti I was transferred to Gorakhpur where I came into contact with Shri Mahavir Prasad Poddar, a great litterateur, a patriot and a social worker.

* * *

Encouraged by the applause which my short stories received, I continued to write. Twenty-five stories were published in an anthology entitled *Prem Pachisi,* followed by thirty-two in *Prem Batisi* and later forty in *Prem Chalisi.* As my short stories were translated and published in Hindi journals, I started writing for the *Saraswati*. I later published several collections in Hindi, including *Sapta Saroj, Nav Nidhi, Prem Pachisi* and several others. In 1918, when I was in Gorakhpur, my major novel *Sevasadan* was published. *Maryada, Abhyudaya, Pratap, Bharat Mitra* and *Saraswati,* all carried excellent reviews of the novel. People thought very highly of this novel in Hindi.

---

* Premchand's first novel was *Asrar-I-Maabid.* It was serialized in the Banaras-based Urdu Weekly, *Avaaz-I-Khalq* from October 1903. It remained incomplete, Premchand seldom referred to it except casually to a writer H. Ghouri who thought it was *Asrar-I-Muhabbat. Kishna,* of which no copy is available, was his second. *Hum Khurma-O-Hum Savab* was his third novel.

But it got me Rs 500 only. The goddess of wealth seemed perched on a high pedestal. I tried to entice her but she did not come down. While I was in Gorakhpur, I passed my B.A. examination.

My ailment continued. On the advice of Poddar and some other friends I tried to cure myself with the 'water-cure'. After three or four months, I felt it affected me adversely. I had a big paunch and when I walked, I felt weak. Once, when along with some friends, I climbed a staircase, I felt my feet would not move. Everyone else rushed upstairs but I literally crawled. That day I felt my weakness acutely.

I felt hurt at the very mention of my illness. Passing through Urdu Bazar, one evening, I met Shri Dashrath Prasad Dwivedi, editor of *Swadesh*. He knew me and we used to exchange ideas on literature. When he saw my condition, he said to me, 'You are absolutely pale, Babuji; you must get yourself treated.'

'I'll die, that's all, isn't it?' I said to Dwivedi with some annoyance. 'I am ready to welcome death.'

Dwivediji felt embarrassed and later I was sorry to have said this.

I became aware that I did not have long to live. I wanted to forget that I was a sick man. If I had only a few months to live, I said to myself, why not live them cheerfully. I gave up the water-cure.

This was in 1920.

TEN

THE JALLIANWALABAGH MASSACRE HAD TAKEN PLACE. NON-cooperation was at its peak. Gandhiji visited Gorakhpur on 16 February 1921. A dais was erected for him in Chowk Ghazimian. The audience numbered at least 200,000, drawn not only from the town but also from the village around. I had never seen such a big crowd in my life. The sight of Gandhiji wrought a miracle in me – a half-dead man – and I got a new lease of life. Three or four days later, I resigned my post – after twenty years of government service. The raison d'etre of the government of any country, as my alter ego Harbilas said in the short story *Red Tape,* is justice and people's rights. If those representing the government do not deviate from this basis, the fall of the government is unlikely. The British government had always held aloft the ideal of justice and had allowed each community and each individual the freedom to act and believe, so long as it did not hurt the other community.

There were people who had devoted their lives to the service of the nation and underwent hardships. I considered myself a greater well-wisher of the nation than most people. What one dedicated official can contribute to the good of the people, I maintained, patriots cannot. However, when one is called upon to work against the welfare and good of the nation, could there be anything more shameful? And should I, for my own selfish end, kill my conscience?

I had lost faith in the intentions of the government. To serve the government was not appropriate. I avoided talking to the children about non-cooperation. The simplest thing would annoy me and when I mentioned non-cooperation to the wife, she disagreed. I didn't wish to tell the children about it, because they would be heart-broken. Every moment of government service was now weighing heavily on me. But my own helplessness stood in the way of resolving my dilemma. The common practice of thousands of traders is to earn their living but I had no professional experience or work to earn a living. I was unfit for anything other than service.

My resignation letter said:

> Sir, it is my belief that God's will is reflected in the conduct of human affairs. His laws are based on truth, mercy and justice. For the last fifteen years, I have served the government and carried out my duties with sincere loyalty and devotion. It is possible that on some occasions some of my superior officers were not satisfied because I have never taken it upon myself to carry out their personal wishes. Whenever there was a conflict between the orders of the superior officer and law, I followed the path of law. I have always understood government service as the best medium to serve the people and country.
>
> Now the government's actions are against my conscience and principles. They interfere, in my view, with truth and justice.

> I am unable to implement them. These orders are an obstacle in the way of the country's independence and constitute an attack on its political awakening. In the circumstances, for me to continue my relationship with the government would be a disservice to the country and to the nation. Along with other rights, the subjects have also the right to wage a political struggle. And as the government is determined to snatch away this right, I, as an Indian, am unable to serve the government. I request, therefore, that I be relieved of my post as soon as possible.

When friends and colleagues heard of the resignation, they tried to persuade me to desist. But I was adamant, and submitted the resignation. Colleagues still thought that the senior officers would not accept it. However, the next day the resignation was accepted. Charge of office was handed over very happily the next morning. As evening approached, however, my enthusiasm disappeared. Worries bothered me. A few hundreds were to be paid to the clothier. The domestic servants had to paid their salaries.

The house rent had not been paid for six months. The milkman and the confectioners' bills were to be paid. Seeing all my creditors gathered was a distressing sight. Accustomed to receiving a monthly salary on a fixed day and making disbursements was a part of life. To meet this expenditure during the course of the month was unusual especially because I did not have the money to disburse. As a last resort, I got the money from the savings bank and distributed it. There was a sizeable dent in the savings pass book. Unlike in the past, when my current bills and their arrears were paid at my convenience, now the total of the current bills and arrears had mounted like the heap of dust that gets exposed from underneath a carpet when it is removed. Many articles of daily use, collected over the years, were auctioned. All these were not needed now. Said my dear wife, 'Why be downcast. It is not a matter to feel sorry about. It is a matter of joy. You are liberated. Besides, this is not the only means of livelihood. When God has made an opening in the mouth he will give something to feed on. If we do injustice, it will visit on your children too. God has wished something good, he gave you this idea.'

I wanted to preach non-cooperation in the villages. Our two families, mine and Poddar's, shifted to his house in the village and took to the manufacture of charkhas.

The end of government service marked the end of my nine-year-old chronic ailment. It made me a complete fatalist, and my firm conviction now is that nothing happens unless He wishes it.

The programme chalked out did not work.

I could not take up farming or weaving. In fact I was not suited for any profession other than journalism, book writing or working in a press. The idea of starting a Urdu weekly from Gorakhpur had been given up because the weekly, *Al-Tahqiq,* which had earlier closed down, had now been revived. With this paper in the field there was no scope for another one to have any circulation.

Back in Banaras, on my return to the house in the village Lamhi, I saw the house was dilapidated. There were weeds all over and around. The villagers had dumped manure and garbage outside the door of the house. For several years, no one had visited the house. Having got accustomed to living in large houses in the cities, being back in the village was a new experience. Work for cleaning up was taken in hand. When the villagers heard of the return of the native, they rushed to say hello...when we had visited the village in the past, everyone was jealous. Now, they were curious and behaved as if they were visiting a museum; then, they dared not ask questions. Not now. I shifted to Banaras and I started serving the villages and literature.

Wrote for the Swadesh *of Gorakhpur and the* Aaj *of Kashi.*

ELEVEN

WHEN THE FREEDOM MOVEMENT GATHERED MOMENTUM, IT reached the villages too. So did the message of non-cooperation; to boycott government offices, schools, colleges and courts and to promote Swadeshi. In one village close by, the population was divided into two camps. One camp was led by Chaudhury and the other one by Bhagat. Enmity between these two leaders went back three generations. Chaudhury was for the freedom movement and Bhagat sided with the other group of those loyal to the British government. Then, a newcomer to the village started a Kisan Sabha. Chaudhury joined his ranks. But Bhagat kept a distance from him.

There was indeed a new awakening in the village and people started talking about Swaraj. Chaudhury was a Swaraj supporter. Bhagat, on the other hand, supported the loyalists. Chaudhury's house became a centre for the Swarajists and Bhagat's house drew the loyalists. Chaudhury started propagating the cause of Swaraj. 'Friends,' he addressed the people, 'Swaraj means our own rule. And isn't one's own rule better than the one by foreigners?'

The people responded, 'Our own is better.'

'I'll tell you,' said Chaudhury, 'how we will get Swaraj. Through our own struggle, our own efforts and through unity. We must all get united and see that we don't discriminate against each other. We must also resolve to settle our differences through discussion.'

Said one dissenter: 'But you are always seen in the courts.'

Chaudhury: 'Yes, I was seen in courts in the past. From this day onwards, if I ever go to a court, I should be considered guilty and punished as if I had slaughtered cows. You should all spend your hard-earned money on your children and the rest on social welfare and charity. Why should you spend any amount on lawyers, their agents or on giving bribes to the police, or be servile before the officials? In the past, our boys were made to inculcate values of our own way of life; they became virtuous, self-sacrificing and hardworking. But today, they go to schools run by foreigners, take up government jobs, accept bribes, live lives of indulgence, run down our gods and goddesses, and are servile before the officials. Isn't it our duty to teach children according to our own way of life?'

People: 'Let us raise money and start our own schools.'

Chaudhury: 'We used to consider drinking a social evil. But today there are liquor shops in every village, nay in every street. We spend crores of rupees of our hard-earned money on alcohol and drugs.'

People: 'Those who drink or take drugs should be punished.'

Choudhury: 'Our ancestors used to wear coarse clothes; they used to spin yarn. As a result, our wealth remained within the country and our weavers could lead lives of ease. But these days we would do anything to be able to put on fine imported clothes.

That's how the foreigners drain wealth from this country. The weavers here have been impoverished. Such being the way of life, our own people are deprived and the foreigners benefit.'

People: 'But coarse clothes are no longer available.'

Chaudhury: 'Wear home-spun clothes and keep away from the courts, and live in peace with others. That, then, is real Swaraj. Those who say that we shall have to shed blood to get Swaraj are mad. Don't pay any heed to what they say.'

The people heard all this with rapt attention. The numbers swelled. They all became admirers of Chaudhury.

Bhagat preached loyalty to the rulers. 'Brothers,' he said, 'our kind king governs this country and the subjects carry out his orders loyally. Our scriptures also teach us loyalty to the ruler. The sovereign, they say, is the representative of God. To disobey his command is sacrilegious. One who is disloyal goes to hell.'

A dissenter: 'Shouldn't the ruler also do his duty towards the subjects?'

Second dissenter: 'Our rulers govern through proxy. The rulers are the traders and merchants sitting far away in England.'

Third dissenter: 'The traders and merchants know how to make money. Why should they be familiar with the rules of administration?'

Bhagat: 'Some people ask you to boycott courts and resolve your problems through the Panchayat. But where are the panches who dispense justice? Who separates the wheat from the chaff? All this, I say, is gimmickry. Those courts decide as per the law and all are equal in the eyes of law – like the lion and the goat drinking water from the same pond.

A dissenter: 'Justice by courts is a sham; it is a sham because only those who have tutored their witnesses and engaged clever lawyers win. And who can distinguish between truth and falsehood? It would certainly be surprising if they did.'

Bhagat: 'We are being told not to use foreign goods. This is a grave injustice. We should buy only what is good and cheap, be it foreign or swadeshi. The money we spend is hard earned and should not be thrown away for third-rate goods.'

A dissenter: 'But money so spent stays within the country, it does not go out.'

Second dissenter: 'The fact that we don't get good food in the house should not mean that you eat foreigners' food.'

Bhagat: 'They advise us not to send our boys to government schools. If our people had not studied in government schools, how would they have got good and high posts or set up big factories? Without access to modern education, we cannot survive in the world today. If you read in the schools of the system of older days, you cannot do anything other than reading horoscopes and reciting scriptures. Will those who read ancient texts be in a position to rule?'

A dissenter: 'We don't have powers to rule. Let us be satisfied with only agriculture. As farmers we are not anyone's slaves.'

Second dissenter: 'Education today makes you arrogant. You put on suits, use watches and walking sticks, put on hats and for one's own whims fill the pockets of foreigners with your own money. It would be better if we remained without such education.'

Bhagat: 'People nowadays are for the use of drugs and drinking alcohol. We all know that drinking is bad. The government today gets crores of rupees as excise from liquor shops. If people could get over these addictions and not go to the liquor shops, it would indeed be good. But if one were stopped from going to the liquor shop, one would buy it through the backdoor at twice or thrice the price and be ready to even face imprisonment – all to meet the needs of addiction. Why take steps to deprive the government of revenue and leave the people impoverished? Also, there are some people who do benefit from drinking. If I miss my dose of opium for a day, my joints suffer form severe pain. I can't breathe and I catch a chill too.'

One voice: 'It is not a good thing that the government should earn money by unfair means. How can living under an irreligious rule do good to the people?'

A second dissenter: 'They make us drink to make us mad and when we get addicted, we require money and is there anyone who gets such high salaries as to afford food, alcohol and drugs? Either you starve your children or you spend money, gamble and become dishonest. And what is a liquor shop but the house of slavishness.'

Such large crowds gathered to hear Chaudhury that there was not enough place to stand. There was a daily accretion to his popularity and there was always serious talk at his house of the progress made by panchayats. People were very happy to participate in these discussions. There was a widening of the people's political thinking. They regained their own pride and sense of importance. They became conscious of their powers too. When they saw injustice and an absence of restraint, they thought of the fruits of freedom, they thought of putting on clothes stitched from home-spun and home-statehood clothes and also home-made food and that justice meted by panchayats was good, and that there would be no fear of the police. With no kowtowing before zamindars' agents, people would be happy and live peacefully. Many people would give up drinking and there would be a feeling of friendliness everywhere.

Bhagat, on the other hand, was not so lucky. People were becoming more and more apathetic to what he said, so much so that except the patwaris, chowkidars, school teachers and friends of government employees, none else came to his meetings. Sometimes senior government officers did come to his meetings to show their support for sometime. Bhagat's tears were wiped but this show of honour for a few moments could not wipe out the dishonour throughout the day. Whichever way he went people raised accusing fingers. Some said, 'there goes the sycophant'; others called him an informer on the payroll of the police.

Bhagat was bitter at the praise lavished on his adversary Chaudhury and felt the humiliations heaped on him. It was the first occasion in his life, he felt, that he had been insulted publicly. All his efforts to keep up the noble name and traditions of his ancestors unsullied, for which he had sacrificed a good deal, had been in vain. This feeling allowed him no peace of mind. He worried incessantly and was keen to find ways to regain his old honour, or to pull down his adversary and make a dent in his pride.

One evening there was a meeting at Chaudhury's doorstep. Farmers from the areas around were attending. There was a big crowd numbering several thousand. On either side there were clusters of women. Chaudhury was speaking of the benefits of Swaraj. There were cries of 'Bharat Mata ki jai'.

Chaudhury finished his speech and took his seat. The volunteers then got down to the job of collecting donations for the Swaraj Fund. Then, out of the blue as it were, Bhagat appeared from somewhere; he stood before the vast gathering and spoke loudly. 'Brothers,' he said, 'don't be surprised to see me here. I am not an opponent of Swaraj. Anyone who runs down Swaraj would be a wretched creature. But the way to achieve Swaraj, I tell you, is not the way which Chaudhury has outlined, and which you all seem enamoured of. If there are differences in our ranks, what can the panchayats do? When people lose themselves in ease and indulgence, how can you make them get over their addictions? And how will you boycott liquor shops? How will you get rid of the habit of smoking cigarettes or of using soaps, socks, vests and underwear? When there is lust for power and influence, how will you abstain from government schools. How will you get over the system of irreligious teaching? There is only one way of achieving Swaraj, and that is by self-discipline. It is this medicine that will root out all the maladies. If you are brave, exercise restraint, control your emotions, you will earn affection. Get over enmities and eliminate jealousies and hatred. Then alone will you get bodily pleasures. And then alcoholism will also end. Without inner strength, you'll never attain Swaraj. Our ego is the basis of all evils. It is this that takes you to the courts and also makes you a victim of irreligious education. Kill this devil with your self-confidence. And then you'll reach your goal. Everyone here knows that for the last forty years, I have been addicted to opium. From this day, I will consider opium as the blood of the sacred cow. My enmity with Chaudhury goes back three generations. From this day, he is a brother to me. From this day, you will see me and Chaudhury as members of one and the same family. And from this day, if you see any member of my family not putting on garments stitched from home-spun and home-woven yarn you may inflict any punishment on me that you wish. That's all that I have to say. May God fulfill your wishes.'

Saying this, Bhagat started for his home. Chaudhury rushed forward and hugged him. The enmity of three generations ended in a few moments. From that day onwards, Chaudhury and Bhagat started preaching the message of Swaraj. There was now a close friendship and it was difficult to know whether the people respected and honoured Chaudhury or Bhagat more. Competition was the spark which lit the heart-lamp in both.

It wasn't easy going to Lamhi and Banaras. I took up the job of headmaster of the Marwari school in Kanpur. I got fed up within a few months and therefore resigned on 22.2.22. The short story Prerna *gives an idea of life at the Kanpur school. Here is the story…*

TWELVE

THE MOST TROUBLESOME PUPIL IN MY CLASS WAS SURYA Prakash. I had never in my teaching career had such a bad student. To play tricks and pranks was his pastime. He took pleasure in making fun of teachers, provoking them and also in harassing well-behaved students. He laid such traps that one wondered at his ingenuity. He organized cliques too, and created a sort of mafia which ruled the school through terror. One could defy the principal of the school, but not Surya Prakash's orders. The peons and other lower staff of the school trembled in front of him.

Once there was to be an inspection of the school. The Principal issued instructions that the students must report to the school half an hour early so that they could be told what to do. At 10 o'clock when the inspector arrived, there was not a single pupil in the school.

At 11 o'clock, the students rushed in like birds who had escaped. The inspector wrote in his report: 'Discipline is poor'. The Principal felt let down, the teachers felt disgraced. And the responsibility was entirely Surya Prakash's. An inquiry was held, but no one dared name Surya Prakash. I had been proud of my knowledge of the rules of school administration. In training college, I had earned a name with regard to the principles of administration, but here all my knowledge was useless. I was at my wit's end to know how to bring this Satan to behave properly. The teachers met several times, but this knot remained entangled. Once there was a move to rusticate Surya Prakash. Fearing that it be construed as a proof of our inability, this move was not pursued. It was indeed a sad reflection that a score of experienced teachers could not discipline a boy of twelve or thirteen years.

While the entire school trembled before Surya Prakash, I was actually at the receiving end because Surya Prakash was in the class that I taught. I had, therefore, to bear the brunt of his pranks. One day, when I pulled the drawer out, a big frog jumped out of the drawer. I retraced my steps and there was commotion in the classroom. I looked at Surya Prakash angrily, and spent a full hour in preaching the good values of life. But he was smiling, his head bent low. I really wondered how he had passed the examinations of the lower classes. Once I lost my composure and told him he would never get promoted. Surya Prakash immediately replied, 'Please don't worry about my passing the examination,' he said. 'In the past I have always passed and this year also I'll pass.'

'Impossible,' I said.

'Impossible will become possible,' he said.

I looked at his face with surprise. Even the brightest student never made such a claim with so much confidence. I thought he must have managed to get advance copies of question papers in the past. I decided that this would never happen again and I would see how many more years he would spend in this class. He might then leave the school. I took special care, therefore, to ensure secrecy of the examination paper. However, when I saw Surya Prakash's answer book, I was surprised. He had scored the highest marks in the class in the two papers that I had set. I had firmly believed that he would not have been able to answer any of the questions asked and I had hoped that I would be able to prove my point. Now, in the face of these answer books, what was I to do? As the handwriting was certainly his, there was no doubt whatsoever on that score. When I spoke to the Principal about this he too was puzzled, but did not wish to any take steps that might cause embarrassment. None of the other teachers showed any concern; according to them there was nothing unusual about the admission of such pupils. To me, however, this pupil was a great mystery. If he continued to misbehave as he did, I thought he would either land himself in jail or a lunatic asylum.

When I left this school (for another one) in the following years I heaved a sigh of relief because Surya Prakash would no longer be a headache for me.

Pupils of my class bade me farewell and came to the railway station to see me off. There were tears in the eyes of all the boys.

Then I suddenly noticed Surya Prakash standing in the last row. I think his eyes were moist too.

I felt like exchanging a few words with him. Maybe he had wished to say a few words to me. But I did not take the initiative. Nor did he. I have always felt remorseful about my wavering. His hesitation was excusable. Mine was not. It is just possible that in that state of compassion and pity, a few sympathetic words might have brought about a change in him. But then such lost opportunities are the substance of life. Anyway, the train started and gathered speed. Some pupils ran alongside the train in motion. I put my head out of the window. For some distance I saw their handkerchiefs waving. Then they dissolved into the distance. I saw there was still one person standing on the platform. I think it was Surya Prakash. At that moment I relaxed my earlier feelings of hatred and disappointment and longed to hug him. But then, in the new place where I would now work and in my new surroundings, memories of the past would fade.

No letter was written nor any received. That perhaps is the way of the world. The greenery of the rainy weather does not last long.

It was a coincidence that I was posted as the Principal of a college. This assignment was indeed a blessing for me. I had never even dreamt that I would rise so high. But the lure of office was such that it inspired me to endeavour for the higher branch of a tree as it were. I got close to the minister concerned. He was kindly disposed towards me. But he did not have even a rudimentary knowledge of educational policies. He, therefore, entrusted the entire responsibility upon me. He was riding the horse and its reins were in my hands. This resulted in his political opponents becoming hostile towards me...I was being attacked without any reason.

I have always been opposed to compulsory education. For, I believe that every man should have a good knowledge of the subject with which he is concerned in his daily life. Compulsory education is necessary in Europe but not in India. Materialism is the basis of western civilization where the principal motivation for all actions is economic profit. The needs of their lives are many and the struggle for life is difficult. Parents are lost in their daily chores and they force their children to start earning as soon as they can. Rather than save a shilling a day, they make the children earn that extra shilling. Life in India is relatively ascetic. Unless circumstances force people to do so, we don't ask our children to start earning. Even the poorest of Indian labourers is enamoured of the benefits of education. He is very keen that his children should get at least an elementary education. He is keen on this not because he thinks that having been educated he would get some powers, but because education is a worthwhile acquisition. It is an equipment for life. This being his outlook, if he is unable to send his children to school it must be because he has no option. In this situation to impose the law that he must send the children to school is, in my opinion, an injustice. Besides, there is a paucity of suitable teachers in this country; you cannot expect half-educated and low-paid teachers to inculcate pupils with high ideals. At the most, four or five-year-old children would learn only the alphabet.

I consider this to be like digging a mountain to find a mouse. Adolescents can learn the same amount in a fraction of the time. On the basis of my own experience, I can say confidently that what an adult can learn in one month's time, a child would not even in three years. What is the advantage in putting children into school, 'which is like a prison'. Outside school, he would get at least fresh air and the benefit of nature's blessings. Actually, by putting the child in a madrasa, you are cutting at the very roots of his mental and physical growth.

When the Bill for making education compulsory was moved by the legislative council, the minister, on my advice, opposed it. The result was the Bill's rejection. This resulted in the vilest criticism of the minister and me. I was the poor man's wife, the butt of ridicule.

There were personal attacks on me. I was considered an enemy and a slave of bureaucracy. I was blamed for all the ills in the school. I had dismissed a peon. Now there was an outcry on this account and he was reinstated. This to me was unbearable. I said to myself, 'Why should my powers to take action or administrative steps be curbed?' There were several other questions asked: Why was a name not sent up for examination? Why was X given a stipend in preference to Y? Why was a particular teacher not allotted a particular class? Such baseless charges against me made me fed up. I decided to resign.

I had hoped that the minister would do me justice in this matter, but he preferred policy to justice and the reward for my years of devoted service of several years was that I was dismissed. Never in my life had I had such a bitter experience.

Several years later, when I was teaching in a small school in a village, the deputy commissioner of the district appeared before me in his car. I was dressed somewhat shabbily and felt embarrassed. However, I stretched out my hand to shake his.

But the young man bent down and put his head on my feet. I was taken aback. The deputy commissioner then raised his head and said to me, 'Sir, perhaps you haven't recognized me.'

My mind's eyes suddenly opened and I said, 'Aren't you Surya Prakash?'

'Yes sir,' he said. 'I am that wretched pupil of yours.'

'That was some thirteen years ago,' I said.

Surya Prakash smiled. 'Teachers forget their pupils, but pupils always remember their teachers.'

Surya Prakash did not know that I had fallen out with the powers that be. And in the same jovial way I said, 'It is impossible to forget pupils.'

Surya Prakash said meekly. 'It is to be pardoned for those mistakes, that I have come to you. I was always interested in your well being. When you went abroad, I wrote a letter of congratulations, but could not dispatch it. When you became a principal, I was ready to go to England. There I used to read your articles in the press. And when I came back to India, I learnt that you had resigned and gone to some village. It is more than a year since I was posted to this district. But I could never imagine that you would be leading this solitary life. How do you pass your days in this desolate village? You seems to have renounced the world prematurely at this young age.'

I cannot say how welcome a surprise this rise in Surya Prakash's life was. If he had been my own son I could not have been happier. I took him into my cottage, and told him my life story.

'In other words,' said Surya Prakash, 'you were stabbed in the back. My own experience is comparatively very short. Within this short time I have seen that we people don't know how to discharge our responsibilities. If I do meet that minister some time, I will ask him if this was how he meted out justice.'

'It is not his fault,' I said. 'It is just possible that placed in his position, I too would have acted in the same manner. I got punished for my own selfishness, and I am grateful to him. This is a fact. I can tell you that I have never had the peace of mind that I have here. It is in the solitude here that I have come to know that in the race for wealth and power, it is not at all possible to have peace of mind. After reading tomes of history and geography and studying in the universities of Europe, I could not get rid of my own ego. In fact this attribute was getting more pronounced and it was becoming unbearable. Without putting your feet on the rungs of the ladder, you can never ascend higher. Greater heights can be achieved only at the cost of others, they being the rungs of the ladder. It is only by trampling them that you can ascend. And there is no place there for courtesy or sympathy. It seems to me now that at the place I then was, I was surrounded by wild ferocious animals, and all my energies were spent in self defence. Here, in this place, I find contentment, commonness and naturalness. Those who come to me here do not expect anything for themselves nor do they lavish praise or my service.'

Having said all this, I glanced at Surya Prakash's face. Instead of a fake smile, there were signs of remorse. Perhaps he had come to me to show that the one I had little hope for is today in this elevated position. Or maybe he had come to elicit praise from me for his great achievement or to make me realize my mistake.

I diverted the talk at once and said to him, 'Do tell me, Surya Prakash, your own life story. How did this transformation come about? If I recall your pranks even today I shudder. Without the blessings of some God, your achievement would not have been possible.'

Surya Prakash smiled and said, 'It was your blessing.'

After a good deal of persuasion Surya Prakash started telling me his life story. 'Several days after you left the school,' he said, 'my cousin, the son of my maternal uncle, came to study in the school. He wasn't more than eight or nine years old. The Principal did not enrol him in the hostel, and my uncle failed to make arrangements for his stay elsewhere. Seeing him in this sad plight, I said to the Principal, "Let the young man stay in my room." The Principal said this was against the rules. That very day, I left the hostel, rented a house, and stayed with my cousin Mohan. Mohan had lost his mother a few years earlier. He was so thin, weak and poor that from the very first day I was sympathetic to him. He always had some illness or the other. Sometimes he had headaches and at others fever. As evening approached, he would start dozing. It was with great difficulty that I made him get up to have his dinner. He was a late riser in the morning, and would not get up till I took him in my lap. At night he would get frightened and jump into my bed. He would go to sleep embracing me. I never lost my temper with him. Why I loved him, I cannot say. While earlier I refused to get up till 9 o'clock, now I got up very early and warmed the milk for him. I would make him get up and have a wash and then have breakfast. In order to make him healthy, I would take him for a morning stroll. I had seldom got down to studying books, but now I would spend hours teaching him. How I became aware of my own responsibilities is a surprise to me. If he ever had any complaint, I was in a panic. I would run to the doctor, get medicines and administer them to Mohan. I was always worried that something that he disliked might happen. For, who else was there but me to make him happy. If any of my naughty friends made fun of him or provoked him, I would be furious. There were many boys who called me an old maid. I would ignore all such jibes. And in his presence I never uttered one inappropriate word, lest he should, following my example, become a bad boy. I wished to lead a life that should be a model for him to follow and for this I would need to reform my own character. Habits such as getting up at 9 o'clock, loitering about till noontime, drawing up plans for new pranks or evading the gaze of a teacher and playing truant were forgotten. Till now, I had been an opponent of all principles and themes of character-building. But now there was no better defender of these than me. Earlier I used to make fun of God, but now there was no greater follower than myself. In all innocence, Mohan would say, "They say that God is everywhere; he should, therefore be with me too." It was impossible for me to treat this lightly, and I would say, "Yes, God is everywhere, with you, with me and with everybody and he protects us all." When he would hear this, his face would brighten. Perhaps he felt the all-embracing power of the Almighty. Within a year, Mohan was transformed. When his father, my uncle, came and saw him, he was taken aback. With tears in his eyes, he said. "You have given him a new lease of life. I had lost all hopes. God will certainly reward you for this. His mother, now in heaven, would certainly be blessing you."'

Surya Prakash's eyes were moist. I said to him, 'Mohan too would have loved you deeply.'

In the tear-filled eyes of Surya Prakash, there was a trace of joy. He said, 'Yes, he would not leave me even for a minute. He would sit by my side, eat with me, and sleep with me. I was his everything. Alas, he is no longer in this world. But I still picture him before my eyes. Whatever I am is entirely because of him. If he had not shown me the path, I would perhaps have been in jail somewhere. One day I told Mohan, "If you don't have a bath everyday, I won't speak to you." The result of my threat was that he would get up early every morning and have a bath. Irrespective of how cold it was, or whether it was windy, he would have a bath. He took note of everything that made me happy. Once I had to accompany some friends to the theatre, and told him to eat on time and go to bed. When I returned at 3 o'clock in the morning, I saw him sitting up. "Why haven't you gone to sleep?" I asked. He said that he couldn't. From that day onwards I never went to the theatre again. The hunger for love in children is so strong that for the comfort of a mother's lap a child would sacrifice the wealth of the world. Mohan's love for me was never satiated. It echoed in Mohan's veins. He was like a creeper ascending along the support it gets and if separated from its support, would break into bits. He stayed with me for three years. Those years were like a ray of light in my life. But he disappeared into the darkness. What ambitions must there have been in that frail body. Perhaps God sent Mohan to me to create a support in my life. When the goal was reached he didn't need to stay any longer.

'During two summer vacations, Mohan stayed with me. Despite his father's wishes, he did not go home. In the third year, however, my college friends decided to go to Kashmir for the summer holidays. They made me the group leader. I had wanted to visit Kashmir for a long time. For this opportunity, therefore, I was grateful to God. I sent Mohan away to my uncle's and went to Kashmir. When I returned after two months, I came to know that Mohan was ill. While I was in Kashmir, I thought of Mohan and even thought of cutting short my holiday. How deeply I loved him became clear to me only during my Kashmir sojourn. But my friends would not allow me to leave. When I heard of his illness, I became restless, and reached him soon. Seeing me, his pale and dried-up face brightened with joy. I rushed to embrace him. The distant look in his eyes and the unusual glow on his face were an indication of his imminent death.

'In an emotionally charged, trembling voice I said, "What a state you are in, Mohan. You have become emaciated in just two months."

'"You had gone only to Kashmir," said Mohan, "and I am going to travel in the heavens."

'I am narrating this tale of woe not to elicit sympathy or to make others feel sorry. After I had gone to Kashmir, Mohan started studying. He was determined to finish one year's study in two months' time, so that when school reopened, he would get my appreciation as his reward. He thought of how I would pat his back, congratulate him, praise him to my friends. All these ideas encouraged his childlike thoughts because of an obsession that possessed him. My uncle was too preoccupied with his office work to find the time to look after him. Maybe he was very happy to see him study. Whenever he saw him play games, he reprimanded him. When he saw Mohan studying there was little he could say. And the result of his being lost in study was that he started getting a little fever. But he did not give up studying. His fever became worse but whenever it came down, he'd pick up his books again.

'Even when his fever was high he would ask the servants whether they had a letter from me and when was I returning. Had I known that this was the price I had to pay for my Kashmir visit, I would not have gone there. I did whatever was possible for me to save him. But he was afflicted with typhoid. It took his life. The dreams of his life became the blessings of a rishi for me. These prompted me, and it was entirely because of him that I have become what I am.

'To make Mohan's childlike aspirations real would have brought me satisfaction and it was this motivation that enabled me to meet the challenges. Otherwise, I am the same stupid Surya Prakash whose face you detested to see.'

I have met Surya Prakash several times since that day. Whenever he visits this area, he never leaves without meeting me. He still considers Mohan his deity. Why this is so is a mystery of human nature that I have not been able to understand.

THIRTEEN

BACK TO BANARAS. EDITED MARYADA *OF THE GYAN MANDAL FOR six months. Then became the headmaster of the school section of the Kashi Vidyapeeth.*

At Kashi Vidyapeeth I was in the service of the nation. While the trouble I faced in the Marwari school at Kanpur was much more than can be imagined, here Babu Bhagwan Das left the school section completely under my charge and did not interfere at all. Initially there was no problem. But when the executive committee decided to abolish the primary school and to merge it with the Kashi Vidyapeeth, I left the school.

I decided to build a house in Lamhi and set up a press in Kashi. When the house is ready, I thought, I'll stay there and return to Kashi everyday. I gave up the idea of living elsewhere. My earnings would not be much, but there would be little danger of loss.

I spent Rs 2000 on the house. Flooring and plastering was yet to be done. Then the plan to set up the Saraswati press materialized. If I had known that the press was to be set up so soon, I would not have started the construction of the house. For the press, I arranged Rs 4000 and requested my cousin (at Indore) to invest Rs 2250 in the press and asked for the same amount from my brother Mahatab Rai. I had hoped that within a year I would be in a position to earn Rs 200 to Rs 250 every month from the press. Contrary to the estimated profit, there were losses. In the first year, far from earning any profit or even paying interest on the investment, the press incurred a loss of Rs 600. I had accepted work from people who could not pay, and it was difficult to realize dues from them. It must have been an inauspicious moment when I became obsessed with the idea of setting up the press. I had enough to live on, but by setting up the press I created a headache for myself. Even my literary work suffered.

Luckily, Dulareylal Bhargava, proprietor of the Ganga Pustak Mala at Lucknow, wanted a publications adviser. I accepted the offer. Bhargava published my Rangabhoomi, *paid me Rs 1800 for it. A Gujarati publisher agreed to pay me Rs 400. I got only Rs 800 for the Urdu edition of* Rangabhoomi. *This amount was small but it was difficult to get any other publisher.*

In the lives of most writers there are occasions when readers write letters of admiration to them. While some praise their style of writing, others are all praise for the nobility of their thoughts. How lucky a writer has been in the recent past is corroborated by other writers. Sitting on tattered blankets, writers can get carried away on waves of pride and self-confidence, forgetting the headaches suffered because of smoke from fires made with green wood, or how mosquitoes and bugs made life impossible. The feeling of self-worth makes them blissful.

In October, I got a letter in which my unimportant books were praised. The writer of this letter was a poet whose poems I had read in a number of journals. Going through his letter, I felt elated and sat down to write back without losing any more time. I have now forgotten what I actually wrote to him. I do recall that my letter was full of affection.

I have not written any poems, nor have I written any poetic work. I did polish the language of my letter so much that when I read it again after I had written it, it gave me the pleasure a poem would have. It was full of emotion. Five days later I received another letter from the poet. It was even more moving than the previous one. In this letter the poet addressed me as 'dear brother' and asked me for a list of my books. It ended with the message that 'my wife is a great admirer of yours and she reads your books with deep interest.' He also said: 'She has asked me to enquire about the place you hail from, and how many children you have. And if you have a photograph of yours, please send it to me.'

This letter gave me great happiness. For, it was perhaps the first occasion when I had heard praise from a female, even though it was through someone else. Now even women had started praising my books. I replied to the letter, using all the adjectives I could think of. My grandfather was the agent of a big zamindar, but I described him as the manager of a princely state. I depicted my father, who was a clerk in an office, as the head of that office. To describe agricultural occupation as zamindari was quite simple. I could not inflate the number of my books but I described how important they were and their popularity and the esteem in which they were held in words which portrayed both my pride and humility.

To praise oneself overtly appears boastful, but by the use of symbolic words it can be done very easily. 'Lovely' can mean its reverse, as 'poor' can mean something entirely different.

My letter was completed and found itself in the letter box. A few relevant remarks from my wife were added in the hope that these would bring the poet and me closer. I had hoped that he would praise my books in one of his own compositions. Then I would outshine others in the field of literature.

For a week there was no reply to my letter. His silence was disappointing. I did not write to him, not wanting him to think I was selfish or sentimental.

Late one afternoon in the month of Ashvin on the occasion of Ramleela, there was a great festivity. I had gone to a friend's house. We were playing a game of cards. Suddenly, a stranger came in, addressed me, and took his seat on a chair next to mine. I was trying to figure out who this gentleman could be and why he had come to see me. My friends who saw him were exchanging peculiar glances.

The man was of medium height and wheatish complexion with pock marks on his face, bareheaded, and his was hair properly combed. He wore an ordinary shirt, a garland of flowers round his neck, boots on his feet, and had a fat book in his hands. I asked him his name. 'They call me Umapati Narayan,' said the stranger. I hugged him; it was the poet with whom I had exchanged letters. I asked him the usual questions, offered him the customary paan and cardamom, and then asked him what brought him here.

'Let us go to your house,' he said. 'I will tell you everything there. I had gone to your house and was told that you were here. I found my way here.'

I went to my house with Umapati. When he was out of the room one of my friends asked me, 'Who is this fellow?'

'A new friend of mine,' I said.

'Beware of him,' said my friend. 'He looks odd.'

'Your impression is wrong,' I told my friends. 'You are prone to judge every person on the basis of his clothes. A man should be judged on the basis of what he really is.'

'Well,' said one of my friends, 'You should know the reality. I am just warning you.'

I did not react to what my friend had said and came home with Umapati. I bought some snacks from the bazaar. We talked. He recited some of his poems. His voice was melodious. I did not understand the poems that he recited but I praised them. I applauded his poems as if there was no better connoisseur of his poems in the world. Later, we went to watch the Ramleela. We had dinner when we returned. He was now going to Kanpur to fetch his wife.

Umapati wished to start a monthly magazine. One publisher was prepared to pay him Rs 1000 for an anthology of his poems but Umapati preferred to get them published first in journals, and later in the shape of a book at his own cost. He was the owner of a big zamindari in Kanpur district but he hated the zamindari system. He wished to live the life of a litterateur. His wife was the principal of a women's college.

We continued to talk till past midnight. I have now forgotten most of what we discussed but I do recall that we chalked out a programme for the future. He had to catch a train at 8 o'clock. I woke up at 7 o'clock and saw that Umapati was already ready to leave.

'Please allow me to go now,' he said 'I'll come again on my way back. But now I have to trouble you a little and wish to be excused.' He continued, 'At 2 o'clock I had woken up and was afraid that I would be asleep when the train left. I kept awake the whole night because I didn't want to miss the train. When I got into the train, I dozed off. When I woke up at Sarai, I found my coat missing. I looked for it but it wasn't anywhere. Somebody must have taken it while I was asleep. This then was the penalty I paid for sleeping. I had kept Rs 50 in the pocket of the coat for expenses during travel. That amount was gone. Please lend me Rs 50 to buy some clothes. I have also to meet some expenses of a few customary rituals at the in-laws' house. These expenses have to be incurred otherwise one looks foolish. I promise to return this amount.'

I was in a real dilemma. I had been cheated once earlier. It occurred to me that I might be taken for a ride again. But then I felt ashamed of myself for lack of confidence in others. Everyone in this world is not the same, I told myself. This poor man is a gentleman. He is now in trouble and I am distrusting him.

I asked my wife, 'Haven't you got some money?'

Wife: 'What do you want it for?'

Myself: 'My friend had his pocket picked. He has to go to his in-laws to fetch his wife. He will repay it on his way back.'

'Most of the people who come to you as friends cheat you. And they are always in trouble,' said my wife sarcastically.

I beseeched her, 'Please give some money. The poor man is standing, ready to depart. He will miss the train.'

'Please tell him that there is no money in the house at this time,' my wife said.

That would mean telling him that I am penniless and without friends, I thought. Could I not manage just Rs 50? It would be better to tell him frankly, 'we don't trust you, and that is why we cannot give you Rs 50.' If we do that, we hide our shame.

Irritated, my wife threw the key to me and said: 'If you could assess people in the same way as you debate, you would have done well in life. Go and give it to him. You'll be able to keep your honour intact. But don't imagine you are loaning it to him; you should know that you are throwing it down the drain.'

At the moment, I was interested, getting the money and not getting lost in arguments. I quietly took out the money and gave it to Umapati. Promising to repay it on his way back, he departed.

Umapati returned along with his wife and daughter. My wife extended to them the customary warm welcome, gave Umapati's wife Rs 20 to mark their first meeting and Rs 2 to their daughter to buy sweets with.

I had thought that Umapati would return the money he had borrowed as soon as he arrived. He did not refer to the subject at all.

Before going to sleep, I said to my wife, 'He hasn't returned the money yet.'

In a tone full of sarcasm, my wife said, 'Did you really think that he would put the money in your hand immediately on his return? I had told you not to give him the money with the hope of getting it back and that you should give it to him with the sole object of helping a friend. But you really are a strange man.'

I kept quiet.

Umapati stayed for two days. My wife extended every hospitality. But I was not at all happy. I thought Umapati had cheated me.

After three days, they got ready to depart. Even at this point, I had hoped he would return the money before they left. However, when I heard his latest yarn, I was stunned. Rolling his hold-all, he said to me, 'I am really very sorry indeed that I haven't repaid the money I had borrowed. You see my father had gone to the villages to realize revenue dues. The villages are not connected by rail line but are accessible only by bullock-cart. That, in fact, is why I stayed only one day at my father's house and then went to the in-law's house where I spent all the money I had. If I had not got the customary farewell money, it would not have been possible to even reach here. Now I don't have money even to buy train tickets.

Please loan me another Rs 25. As soon as I reach my house, I shall send it to you. As a matter of fact, I don't even have money to pay for the ekka to the railway station.'

I felt like ticking him off, but I could not be discourteous. I went again to plead with my wife for money for Umapati. This time, without any arguments, she gave me the money which, somewhat despairingly, I gave to Umapati. His wife and daughter had already gone downstairs; he picked up his hold-all and bade me goodbye. I continued to sit; I did not go outside to bid them goodbye.

A week later, Umapati wrote to say that he was off to Berar for a week, and would send the money on his return from there. A fortnight later, I wrote to him asking him about his well-being. There was no reply. Another fifteen days passed and I wrote to him asking him to return the money he had borrowed. Again there was no reply. Another month passed before I sent him a reminder. This was sent to him under registered post. There is little doubt that he would have received it. Yet, he did not reply. I now agreed with what my wife had said.

Disappointed, I kept quiet over this subject. I did not tell my wife about the letters that I had sent. Nor did she mention the subject.

To my being cheated, everyone with a similar experience has the same reaction. Howsoever noble one may be, one cannot remain unaffected. One may say to oneself, 'I have done my duty; if the debtor has not cared to repay, what can I do about it?' But I am not so generous. I work hard, wield my pen and then only do I see some cash flow in.

Just the other day, a new compositor came to work in my press. He appeared to be efficient. I engaged him at the rate of Rs 15 per month. He had been a student in some school run on Western lines and had left it during the non-cooperation movement.

His family refused to help him in any way. He was then forced to take up this profession. He was only seventeen years old. He was thoughtful and spoke well. Three days after he joined work with me, he was down with fever. For three or four days he remained sick. As the fever continued, he got worried and felt homesick. Wouldn't his people get him treated at least? He came to me and said, 'Sir, I am sick. If you give me some money, I'd like to go home. As soon as I reach there, I will send the money.'

The young man was really sick. I thought well of him. I also knew that he would not be able to get treated here. He needed some help.

But I was apprehensive that he too would dupe me. When an intellectual and a scholarly person could cheat me, how can one trust a semi-literate young man to carry out his promise? I was indeed in a dilemma for a few minutes. Then I said, 'I am really sorry to see you in this situation, but I will not be able to help you. I have no money.'

Hearing me turn down his request, tears rolled down from his eyes and he said, 'If you wish to help me you certainly can arrange for the money. As soon as I get home I'll send you the money.'

I said to him, 'Your intentions today are good. But where is the proof that your intentions won't change after you get home. Who knows whether you will be in a position to send the money back. And there would be no way for me to recover it from you. There is not the least doubt about your intention but I am sorry – I don't have any money at the moment. You can certainly take the wages due to you.'

He did not react like a simpleton. He looked up towards the sky and went away.

I felt a deep remorse, almost hatred, for my selfishness and yet I stuck to the position I had taken. The thought that I was not a wealthy man who could throw money down the drain gave me solace. This then was the result of having been cheated by the poet friend.

I did not know what the result of my actions would be. The situation did not arise. For, it was God's wish to save me from that ignominy. When he left me with tears in his eyes, he met Pundit Prithvi Nath, a clerk in my office. The Pundit asked him how he was.

Hearing his tale of woe, the Pundit, without any hesitation took out Rs 15 and gave it to him. He had borrowed the money from the imprest of the press. When I came to know of what had transpired I felt a great burden off my chest. The young man would now reach his home more easily. I got this satisfaction gratis.

I had felt ashamed of my own meanness. For, I preached compassion, pity, humaneness and good actions in the articles I wrote. When the occasion to do what I preached arose, I had managed to wriggle out of the situation. On the other hand, this poor clerk was so large-hearted and compassionate. The disciple had overshadowed his master. It was also a matter of ironic solace that my own preaching did not have any influence on me but influenced others. There was darkness beneath the lamp but at least it shed light. If the Pundit did not get the money back I would compensate him. But I did not need to; for, five days later, the money was received.

I had never experienced such an eye-opening deed. It was indeed good luck that I did not mention this episode to my wife. For otherwise it would not have been possible for me to stay in my own house. However, I wrote about what had happened and sent it to a periodical. I wanted to portray the bad results of deceitful behaviour. I did not hope that it would have a good effect. But after four days, I suddenly received Rs 75 by money order. I was greatly pleased. The sender of the money was the poet Umapati.

On the counterfoil of the money order was inscribed only one word: 'Forgive'.

I received the money, took it to my wife and showed her the counterfoil.

'Please go and put it back in the box,' she said. 'It has become clear to me how acquisitive you are. To be after somebody so ruthlessly for a small amount is not the quality of a gentleman. If an educated and civilized person does not keep his word, one should understand that he is helpless and there is no need to humiliate a helpless man with reminders. Nobody, unless he is morally fallen, would cheat anybody. I will not take this money, until you get a letter from Umapati explaining why he delayed repaying the money.'

However, I was not prepared to listen to such sane and liberal advice. I had got the money that I had thought had been lost and was supremely happy.

FOURTEEN

When Mahatma Gandhi, in the wake of the Chauri Chaura incident, called off the non-cooperation movement, the struggle for national liberation got a setback. The British government utilized this lull to aggravate Hindu–Muslim differences by managing stone-throwing into Hindu temples and playing music in front of Muslim mosques. Wrote a story Mandir and Masjid.

Chaudhury Itrat Ali was a big jagirdar of Kade. His ancestors had faithfully served the British government and he was awarded this jagir to recognize the services rendered. With his able management he had extended it so much, that there was none in that region as eminent or as wealthy as the Chaudhury. When the British officials toured the area, they always called on him. But Chaudhury saheb never called on any official no matter how high his rank, even if he was the commissioner. It also seemed that he had taken a vow not to go to court. Nor did he attend the darbars or any other official function. He considered it below his dignity to stand with folded hands before officials and acquiesce to every utterance of theirs. As far as possible, he avoided getting involved in legal suits, even if he incurred monetary loss. He had left all his affairs to his agents; it was for them to multiply his assets or to waste them. The Chaudhury was a scholar of Arabic and Persian. He adhered to all that was laid down in the Shari'at; he considered taking interest a sin, did namaaz five times a day, observed fasts on all the thirty days of Ramzan and recited the Quran everyday. There was no place for religious narrow-mindedness in his life. A bath in the Ganga was his daily routine. Rain or cold, he would get up at 5 a.m., every morning, and walk a mile to the banks of the Ganga. Before returning he would fill his big silver jar (surahi) with Gangajal.

He drank nothing but Gangajal. Few yogins or yatis had greater faith in Gangajal than the Chaudhury. Every seventh day his house was cleaned and plastered with cowdung. In his orchard, a Brahmin priest recited the Durga path through the year. And the respect and honour bestowed by him on the sadhus and sanyasins as would have been the envy of kings. Free food was served to all on a permanent basis. Muslim fakirs were served food cooked in a special kitchen. Over 100 guests ate at his table everyday. Yet, in spite of all this charity he owed not a penny to any mahajan. He was blessed, and his assets grew steadily day by day.

It was well known throughout his estate that for cremations, yagnas, community feasts or marriages, the trees in his estate could be felled without any permission; even the Chaudhury's permission was not necessary. On the occasion of the marriage of any Hindu in his realm, he was always represented by someone or the other. The amount he gave as presents was fixed. The amount contributed towards weddings of daughters was fixed. Besides elephants and horses from his stable, his tents and shamianas, palanquins, carpets, fans, liquor and silver utensils were loaned without any fuss. One had merely to ask for them. So well-known for his charity and large-heartedness was the jagirdar that all his subjects were ready to sacrifice their lives for him.

Chaudhury saheb had in his employment one Rajput called Bhajan Singh, who was his chaprasi. The six-feet-tall, broad-chested Bhajan Singh walked proudly through crowds. Fear was unknown to him. Chaudhury saheb had such faith in him that when he went for his Haj he took him along.

There was no dearth of those inimical to the Chaudhury. Nearly all the zamindars in the neighbourhood were jealous of his fame and power. Because of him, they could not oppress their ryots; for they knew that he was always ready to stand by them. The Chaudhury, with Bhajan Singh accompanying him, was not afraid of even sleeping at the doorsteps of his enemies. On several occasions he was surrounded by foes, but Bhajan Singh, risking his own life, brought him to safety. However, if he went out and did not return in time, the Chaudhury would get apprehensive fearing that he might have got embroiled in a fracas. For his condition was like that of a domesticated ram which when released from the chain, runs to lock horns. As for Bhajan Singh, there was none in the world to equal his Chaudhury saheb.

The Muslims in the area were jealous of the Chaudhury. They thought that he had bid farewell to the ways of Islam. They could not understand his philosophical principles. If he was a good Muslim, they asked, why should he drink Gangajal, give respect to sadhus or arrange the Durgapath? They hatched plans against him and also made plans to harass the Hindus. They had decided to attack the Thakurdwar (temple) on Janmashtami. The Hindus were browbeaten and told if they had thought their power was derived from Chaudhury saheb's support, they were mistaken.

After all, what could the Chaudhury do? If he sided with the Hindus he would be taken care of and all his bias in favour of Hindus would be countered.

On a dark night, Lord Krishna's birthday (Janmashtami) was celebrated in the Thakurdwar at Kade. An old toothless man was singing dhrupad on a tanpura. The other bhaktas awaited the completion of the raga, so that they could start their kirtan on the drums and cymbals. The cook was preparing food for the crowd. Hundreds of people had gathered to watch the programme.

Suddenly a group of Muslims armed with lathis appeared on the scene and pelted stones at the temple. There was an uproar. Who was throwing them, asked some. Others went outside to see what was happening. The Muslims were ready. They rained lathis. The Hindus had nothing except drums and cymbals. Some took shelter in the temple while others fled in different directions. There was noise everywhere.

Chaudhury saheb got the news. 'Thakur,' he said to Bhajan Singh, 'go and see what all this clamour is about. Tell the villains to behave. And if they don't do so, handle them firmly. But see that there is no bloodshed.'

The Thakur, who had heard the uproar, was grinding his teeth in anger. He had exercised self-restraint. The Chaudhury's orders were like a boon he'd asked for. He placed his mighty staff on his shoulders and rushed to the temple. There he saw the havoc the Muslims had played. They had pushed many people into the temple and were breaking glass panes. His eyes bloodshot, the Thakur was beside himself with anger. He challenged them, entered the temple and started hitting them. On one side was the lone Thakur and on the other were some fifty-odd people. But he managed to scare the adversaries who fled.

In his fury, the Thakur did not care for the life and death of others. No one could explain the source of his energy. He felt that some divine force was guiding him. In the dharma yuddha mortals do incredible things.

The Chaudhury, apprehensive that the Thakur might kill somebody, rushed to the temple. There it was all panic. He saw the villains running for their lives. One man was writhing in pain and others were crying. He was about to call out for the Thakur when he saw someone rush towards him and collapse. The Chaudhury saheb recognized him. He reeled back in horror. It was his own son-in-law, Shahid Hussain, the one designated to succeed him.

The Chaudhury shouted for the Thakur, 'Come here, Thakur,' he said. 'Bring a lantern… a lantern… this is Shahid.'

The Thakur panicked. He came with a lantern and saw that Shahid's head was cut and blood was oozing out.

'Thakur, you have blown out the light out of my life,' said the Chaudhury, beating his head in despair. Trembling, the Thakur replied, 'God alone knows that I did not recognize him.'

'No,' said the Chaudhury, 'I am not blaming you. Nobody is permitted to force his way into the abode of God. The misfortune is that the last trace of my family is obliterated and that too at your hands! You, who were ready to sacrifice your life for my sake. Look at the irony – it is through you that God has ruined me.'

The Chaudhury was weeping bitterly.

The Thakur was very remorseful. He could not have felt worse if his own son had been killed.

'I ruined one for whom I was prepared not just to sweat but to shed my blood for, one who was not just my master but a god, one at whose bidding I was prepared to jump into the fire!' he said. In a hoarse voice, 'Who could be more unfortunate than myself? Today my face has been blackened.'

Saying this, the Thakur took out his knife and was about to stab himself.

The Chaudhury snatched the knife from his hands.

'What are you doing, Thakur?' he said. 'Be sensible. All this is in the hands of fate. It is no fault of yours. What has happened is what God has decreed. If I had forced my way into the temple and desecrated the divine and even if recognizing me, you had killed me, I would have forgiven you. For, there is no greater sin than sacrilege. God is my witness when I say that I don't have anything against you. Had I been in your place, I too would have done the same thing, even if it had been my master's son. My people will pass sarcastic remarks, my daughter will ask me for revenge and all the Muslims in the area will be after my life. I will be called a kafir and an atheist. Some fundamentalists will be ready to kill me. But I will not turn my face away from justice. It is dark outside, please run away fast and hide in some cantonment in my area...I see many Muslims approaching in this direction. I even see members of my own family. Run, I say, run.'

Bhajan Singh stayed incognito for a year on Chaudhury saheb's estate. The Muslims continued searching for him. So did the police. But the Chaudhury shielded him. He bore the brunt of sarcasm, suffered the apathy of his relatives, warded off the probe by the police and faced threats from the mullahs. But no one could find Bhajan Singh. In his lifetime, the Chaudhury would not turn over a dedicated loyal employee to the cruel hands of the law. Several searches were carried out in the cantonments in his jagir. The mullahs tried to win over the Chaudhury's servants, females and musclemen. The Chaudhury succeeded in keeping Bhajan Singh hidden.

Bhajan Singh felt sorrowful about the troubles that Chaudhury saheb was facing to save his life. He thought several times of going to him and saying, 'Please hand me over to the police.' But the Chaudhury reiterated his orders that he remain in hiding. He toured his jagir often and stayed at home only for brief periods.

This was the only way to escape the vitriolic comments of his relatives.

One winter evening, when Chaudhury saheb had retired after dinner, Bhajan Singh suddenly entered and stood before him. He had changed so much that Chaudhury saheb was taken aback.

'Are you all right, Master?' the Thakur asked the Chaudhury.

The Chaudhury replied, 'Yes, thank God, I am all right. But you have changed beyond recognition.'

'Master, it is no longer possible for me to live incognito,' said the Thakur. 'If you approve, I will surrender to the court. Fate will decide my case. I cannot bear to see the worries you are going through.'

Chaudhury: 'No, Thakur, no. So long as I am alive, you will not do anything of the sort. I cannot throw you to the wolves. The police will arrange for the witnesses to say what they want them to and you will have to pay with your life. You have faced grave dangers for my sake. If I cannot do even this much for you, would there be a more ungrateful man than myself? You are never to mention this subject to me again.'

Thakur: 'Master, has someone told you that...?'

Chaudhury: 'Don't worry about this. So long as God wills it, no harm will ever come to me. Please go now. It is dangerous for you to stay here any longer.'

Thakur: 'Master, I hear that people avoid meeting you.'

Chaudhury: 'It is good if my enemies keep away.'

What the Thakur had apprehended was correct. The meeting with the Chaudhury made his resolve all the more firm. 'The Master has been going from pillar to post only for my sake. And no one is ready to stand by him. Indeed anyone could come and attack him any time. I am disgraced.

The next morning, the Thakur reached the house of the district magistrate.

'Where have you been all these days? Was it at the instance of the Chaudhury?' he asked.

Thakur: 'Not at his instance, Sir. I was hiding only because of the danger to my life.'

When Chaudhury saheb heard of the Thakur's surrender he was shocked. What would happen now? If the case was not contested, it would be difficult to save the Thakur's life. And if he contested the case, there would be great agitation in the Muslim world. Fatwas would be issued.

The Muslims of the area had indeed decided that they would see the Thakur hanged. They raised subscriptions. The mullahs in the mosques too appealed for funds, and went from door to door to get donations. The case was given a communal hue. Muslim lawyers got a chance to earn fame, and they started coming from all over to take part in the jihad.

Chaudhury saheb was determined to defend the Thakur, no matter what sort of trouble he would have to go through. The Thakur, according to Chaudhury saheb, was innocent. And he was known not to be afraid of defending the innocent. He left his house and went and camped in the city. He went about the task like a hurricane.

For six months the Chaudhury fought the case. Money flowed like water. He did things which he had never done before and would never do again. He begged touts, entreated lawyers and gave nazars to officials.

The Thakur was acquitted. Anyone who heard about this was surprised. They thought it was indeed noble of the Chaudhury to have saved his servant from the hangman's noose.

However, communal elements saw this in an entirely different light. While the Muslims were furious, the Hindus celebrated. The Muslims felt that this was the end of whatever was left of their creed; the Hindus felt that now was the time for bringing the

Muslims back to the Hindu fold. The mullahs raised their voices for propagating the message of the Prophet; the Hindus, too, raised the standard of unity. Islamic ideology was awakened, so was Hindutva among the Hindus.

The Thakur was swept off his feet. He became the leader of the Hindus. Never in his life had he poured water over the Shiva idol. But now he was ready to wield the lathi in the interest of Hindu gods and goddesses. Although he could not persuade a single Muslim to join the Hindu fold, he did convert two chamars. Some other employees of the Chaudhury also came under his influence. Those Muslims who seldom stood before a mosque now started doing namaaz five times a day. And those Hindus who never peeped into a temple now did sandhya twice a day.

The Hindus in Kade were in a majority. Bhajan Singh became their leader. Awe of his lathi was universal. The Muslims of Kade, even though in a minority, were the dominant group because the Hindus were neither organized nor united. Now that they were well organized and united, how could a handful of Muslims dare confront them?

A year later Janmashtami was celebrated once again. The Hindus had not forgotten the thrashing they had got. Preparations were on in secrecy. The faithful had started gathering in the temple early morning. All of them had lathis in their hands. There were many who had kept knives hidden around their waists.

It had already been decided that there would be some provocation, followed by a fight with the enemy. Never before had a procession been taken out at the time of this festival. On this occasion, however, it was decided to take out an impressive procession.

The lights were on. The evening namaaz was being performed in the mosque. The procession which was taken out had elephants, horses, flags and bands. The procession was led by the proud Thakur Bhajan Singh who was accompanied by many people from his wrestler's ring. The procession came close to the Jama Masjid. The wrestlers wielded their lathis. Everyone was alert. Those who were scattered all over congregated. There were some whispers. The band sang louder and louder. There were victory cries. The procession was now in front of the mosque.

Suddenly one Muslim came out of the mosque and said, 'This is namaaz time. Stop the music.'

Bhajan Singh replied, 'The music shall not be stopped.'

Muslim: 'It will have to be stopped.'

Bhajan Singh: 'Why don't you stop your namaaz?'

Muslim: 'Don't base your audacity on Chaudhury saheb's support. This time you will be brought back to your senses.'

Bhajan Singh: You may base your pride on Chaudhury saheb's strength. We depend upon our own strength. The issue now is one of religion.'

Some more Muslims came out of the mosque and insisted that the music be stopped. However, the music became louder. Matters came to a head. One maulvi called Bhajan Singh a kafir. Upon this, the Thakur pulled his beard. There were scuffles, followed by attacks.

The Thakur gave the war cry. The Hindus advanced and entered the mosque. They fought inside. It is not clear who won. The Hindus said they had hounded and beaten up the Muslims. The Muslims said that the Hindus had been given such a beating that they would never again dare repeat this behaviour. All conceded that Bhajan Singh had displayed unbelievable bravery. The Muslims said that if the Thakur had not been there, no Hindu would have been left alive. The Hindus said that the Thakur was really a reincarnation of Hanuman and his lathi repulsed all attacks by the Muslims.

The function was over. Chaudhury saheb was sitting in his audience room and smoking his hukkah. His face was red and tense. His eyes looked like they would emit fire. The abode of God had been desecrated! The very thought wrenched his heart. Wasn't the vast space in the maidan near the mosque enough for them to fight each other? This spilling of blood inside the abode of God? A temple too is the abode of God. If the Muslims were guilty of desecrating the temple, weren't the Hindus, too, guilty of the same crime? And the pity was that inside the mosque this had been carried out by the Thakur. For such desecration, he had killed my son-in-law. If I had known that he would be responsible for such an act, I would have allowed him to be hanged. Why did I need to go through an ordeal, earn a bad name and seek obligations? The Thakur had been my faithful servant. He had saved my life several times. He was ready to shed his blood for me. But now that he has desecrated the abode of God, he should be punished for it. And what should be the punishment? Well, only hell. Nothing, except the fires of hell could be his punishment; one who has desecrated the abode of God has insulted God.

Suddenly, he saw that Bhajan Singh had come and stood before him. Fixing his gaze on the Thakur, the Chaudhary with great anger asked him, 'Tell me, did you enter the mosque?'

Bhajan Singh: 'The maulvis, Master, attacked us.'

Chaudhury: 'Please answer my question. Did you or did you not enter the mosque?'

Bhajan Singh: 'When they started pelting stones from within the mosque, we entered the mosque to catch them.'

Chaudhury: 'Do you know that a mosque is the abode of God?'

Bhajan Singh: 'I do, Master, of course I do.'

Chaudhury: 'A mosque is as much the abode of God as a temple is.'

Bhajan Singh: 'I did not respond.'

Chaudhury: 'If any Muslim attempts to desecrate a temple, it is a sacrilege. When a Hindu desecrates a mosque that too is sacrilege.'

Bhajan Singh was speechless. He had never seen the Chaudhury so angry.

Chaudhury: 'You killed my son-in-law, and I fought the case to defend you. Do you know why I did this? It is because I considered my son-in-law guilty of an act for which you rightly punished him. If you had killed my son, or even me for such an act of desecration, I would not have asked you for your blood. And today you are guilty of the same desecration. If some Muslims within the mosque had sent you to hell, killed you, I would have been happy. But then like a shameless person, you escaped from there. Do you think that God will not punish you for this sacrilege? It is God's command that he who insults him should be beheaded. To do that is the duty of every Muslim. If a thief is not punished, does it mean that he is not a thief? Do you or do you not agree that you insulted God?'

The Thakur could not deny his guilt. His association with the Chaudhury had distanced him from the bigoted ones. 'Yes, Sir,' he said, 'I am guilty.'

Chaudhury: 'Are you then ready to receive the same punishment that you have given to others?'

Thakur: 'I did not kill your son-in-law knowingly.'

Chaudhury: 'If you had not killed him, then I would have killed him myself. Do you understand what I am saying? No, I will take revenge for the insult to God that you are guilty of. Would you accept this punishment at my hand, or prefer to get it from a court of law? The law court would punish you with imprisonment for some time only but I will put you to death. You have been my friend, but I shall have no remorse. How deeply I have been hurt, only God knows. I will now behead you. That is the command of my religion.'

And saying this, the Chaudhury took out his sword and faced the Thakur. It was a strange spectacle. An old man with his hair grey, his back bent, stood before a giant of a man. The Thakur could have, with just one blow of his lathi, killed him. But he bent his head. He was grateful to the Chaudhury with every pore of his being. He had never imagined the Chaudhury to be so devout. Perhaps he had thought that the Chaudhury was a Hindu at heart. How could be ever think of violence or revenge against the one who had saved him from the gallows? He was a brave man and like all brave men, was without any deceit. At this moment he was far from angry, only full of reproach. He was not afraid of death, but was full of remorse.

The Chaudhury faced the Thakur. His faith told him to kill this man. But the innate goodness of the man told him, 'leave him.' The conflict was between faith and dharma.

The Thakur saw the dilemma the Chaudhury was in. In a choked voice, he said, 'Compassion, Master, would not allow you to raise your hand. You cannot kill the man whom you have brought up. My head is at your service. It is yours. You have saved it and you can take it back. This is yours; I am merely its custodian, and you will get it back. Please send someone to my house tomorrow morning to collect it. For if you behead me here, there will be trouble. If I kill myself at home none would know who killed me. Please forgive me, Master, for whatever lapses I have been guilty of…'

And, saying this, the Thakur left.

The communal clashes formed the background of the next important novel Kayakalp.

Back in Kashi the press continued to be a headache.

The Mahajan from whom Mahatab Rai had borrowed money was pressing him to pay him the interest. My cousin (in Indore) wanted his money back. He had given money to farmers and was getting interest at the rate of two per cent per month. He now felt that investment in the press was a risk, and wanted his money back. I told him the press was incurring losses. He advised me to close down the press and return the money.

As I could not depend upon work from outside, I decided to undertake publishing work. The machine in the press, I reckoned, would print off 2000 copies of one form. Taking into account the holidays, it would print twenty-four forms every month. I'll get twelve forms printed in my press and another twelve from outside, I thought. I also wished to bring out a series of books priced at 10 annas each. Perhaps one book would be out every two months, and I'd get Rs 400. This would take care of the printing of the books. I also planned to publish a series of books, *Sansar Darshan,* on the lines of *Peeps at Many Lands*. This field was untapped and I thought it was badly needed.

I published *Kayakalp, Azad Katha, Prem Tirtha, Prem Pratima, Pratigya.* The sales were poor. I got only Rs 600.

Meanwhile the proprietor of Naval Kishore Press, Bishan Narain Bhargava offered the post of Editor of Madhuri. *I accepted it.*

FIFTEEN

THE MADHURI *FLOURISHED. A CASE FOR DEFAMATION FILED BY one Saligram Shastri increased its popularity, The journal encouraged many young writers, including Jainendra Kumar and Upendra Nath Ashk.*

However, once I received a letter in the name of literature. I was asked to give the foreword to a play. The letter touched me and this was my first contact with the author. Knowing of the deplorable state of literature (and experiencing it), I had no hesitation in obliging him. I wrote to him immediately and asked him to send the play. I got it within a week. His request was not only for a foreword, but also for appointing a publisher. I don't get involved with publishers because in the past my efforts earned me the enmity of several friends. I went through the play, wrote the foreword and returned the manuscript. The play impressed me and

I praised it in the foreword I wrote I have written forewords to many books in the past, and there was nothing unusual about being asked to write another. However, in this case, this was not the end of the matter. Within a week, I received an article for publication in my journal. I generally trust people, more so if it concerns a request from a writer.

On the other hand, I have a friend who keeps a safe distance from even the shadow of a writer. He's a noted writer and a thorough gentleman and is full of life. Whenever I have run into him after his marriage, he has said to me, 'The present for you is kept safe, and I will be sending it to you.' However, I have yet to receive it, even after there have been additions to his family. A letter from this writer contained entreaties and persuasion and indicated the esteem he held me in so that, even though I had not met or seen Mr Joshi, I in turn respect him.

I was told that he was the son of a well-known and a well-to-do person and that he fell out with his father after his uncle had insisted on a huge dowry for him. He didn't acquiesce. The uncle then threw him out of the house. His father cared more for fraternal ties and did not like to hear anything against his brother. What could this idealistic young man do except leave his home? He had to run from pillar to post and finally landed in Gwalior. Here he was stricken with fever and indigestion. He narrates his tale of woe, relates how he faced his troubles with determination and courage and was always ready to work hard – you would certainly have wanted to extend him help.

After several days, Joshi wrote a letter from Allahabad, telling me that he had accepted an assignment in a monthly magazine. I cannot describe how happy I was on receiving this letter. He must indeed be a very hard working man, I said to myself. And my affection for him went very far. The managing editor of the magazine, I was told, was a very hard taskmaster. If Joshi was a little late, the managing editor would deduct a day's salary, and also take him to task. Lost in work this devotee of truth put up with every humiliation. How could he give up this chance to make his future better. His dedication enhanced my trust and esteem for Joshi. But Joshi could not last long in Allahabad and wrote to me that he was prepared to undergo hardships, even starve, but was not prepared to lose his self-respect or hear taunts.

A week later, Joshi wrote to me again to tell me how his employer's behaviour had been unbearable and that he had resigned. 'Please don't think that I have resigned the job on a whim,' he wrote 'I did all that I was expected to do. I did even that which was not expected of me. But I could not sacrifice my self-respect. If I could do that, I would not have left home. I have now decided to go to Bombay to try my luck there. I am determined not to stretch my hand for help from my people. I am prepared to work even as a coolie, but I will not sell my soul.'

I was touched when I read this letter. The writer of the letter was not a character from a play whose joys and sorrows I could be a spectator to. He was now so close to me that I felt that if he were being subjected to an attack I would go to defend him. I was anxious to hear from him from Bombay.

'Nothing to worry about,' he wrote from Bombay. 'I am prepared to face all hardships.' He wrote to me again after a few days, repeating that he was prepared to face all odds, despite the fact that he had been starving for three days.

'What a great idealist,' I said to myself. 'How noble this person is. I think I was hard on him initially.' My inner self said to me, 'Shame on you. Look, he is facing all these troubles alone. Why don't you send him some money. I did not do what my conscience dictated. But I certainly felt remorseful at my stone-heartedness.

I learnt that Joshi had got an assignment in the editorial department of a weekly. I heaved a sign of relief and thanked God.

His weekly published his articles I read them and found them lively and thoughtful. I felt proud of him. He requested me for articles, but I did not have the time to write for his weekly. I felt sorry that I could not write for him and give him encouragement.

It seemed as if problems chased him. The weekly did not have too many subscribers. The paper depended largely on donations. When the paper got some money, it was shared by the employees; otherwise they all worked, waiting for money to come in. He had thought he would get his salary for three months in a lump sum. But the proprietor closed the paper. The employees left in desperation. Joshi drew a blank. There was not the least doubt about the proprietor's goodness. The employees were prepared to work for him on half their salaries, but it was not possible to work on empty stomachs. Life in Bombay is very hard. Poor Mr Joshi had to look for a job again. I felt sorry after reading his letter.

But God did not bless me with the resources to help him. If I had had the means, Joshi would not be going in circles for a livelihood. This time, he did not have to face much difficulty. He had got a job in a textile mill. His job was putting down the numbers on the bundles. His daily wage was a rupee a day, but a rupee in Bombay can buy you what a quarter rupee would get you in northern India. How could he live on a rupee a day?

After several days, I got another letter from him. In this letter he told me that a foreign firm had agreed to employ him only if he could give Rs 100 as security. The firm supplied shoes, soap, cigars, etc., to the armed forces. If he could get this job he could live comfortably for the rest of his life. He said he was fed up with the life he had been leading. There was no hope for him and he felt like committing suicide. 'I worry about my mother,' he wrote. 'If I die, she would weep to death. With my father she has all the comforts of life, but her soul would pine for me. My only wish is that I set up a place of my own, call her here and serve her. I want nothing else in life. But where could I get the Rs 100 for security from? And tomorrow is the deadline; the day after, the candidate next on the list will deposit the security and get the job, and I'll still be waiting. The agent wishes to give me the job, but he has to go by the rules.'

This letter helped me to overcome my proclivity to thriftiness. I realized that where there is a will, there is a way. I decided to send him the money. If this could help a young man, why should he look elsewhere? And could there be a better use for money? Pen-pushers in Hindi normally do not have this sum of money, but I happened to have the money in my purse. The credit for this, of course, goes to my habit of thrift. I consulted my wife. She agreed willingly. As this money was required urgently and a money order would have taken a few days, I went to the telegraph office and sent it telegraphically.

The pleasure I felt would be appreciated only by those who have saved over a long period and faced an uncertain future. Seth Aminchand could not have derived as much happiness after a donation of Rs 100 lakh as I got after sending the Rs 100. Though I had given this amount ostensibly as a loan, it was the repayment of a debt for friendship. And I will never forget the letter of thanks that I received after four days. Each word in the letter was soaked in gratitude. How genuine his words were.

Joshi was staying in a well-known place in Bombay. With his name and the post-box number, the letter could reach him. He wrote several letters to me. He was happy. He wrote that the agency with which he worked was happy with his work and had posted him to Kashi, and that he would be reaching Kashi soon. In addition to his salary, he would also get an allowance. His mother's sister and her husband, a well-known physician, were in Kashi, but he would not like to stay with them. Instead, he would stay separately.

However, he got fed up in Kashi after a month. He now started complaining and narrating his grouses. He said he was made to flatter the army officers till the evenings. He would return after 10 o'clock at night, to a house without lights and no one to talk to or share his happiness with.

'I am bored stiff of eating food in restaurants,' he said, 'I had hoped that I would pass my days in peace. But it looks like I will have to continue to struggle hard. No, I cannot live this life any longer. I spend the nights weeping.'

From these letters I felt Joshi was slipping down from his ideals. I wrote to him, advising him not to resign. He wrote back saying that he could not stay in the job any longer. 'The armymen's behaviour is unbearable,' he said. 'And the manager is now transferring me to Rangoon. If I do go to Rangoon this would mean the end of me.' Joshi also told me, 'I wish to serve literature and be with you for some time.'

Before I could send a reply to his letter, he wrote to me that he would be reaching by the Dehra Dun Express. And the next day he actually arrived.

He was a frail man, dark complexioned, with a longish face and big eyes, and was dressed in European attire. He had several leather boxes, a suitcase, and a holdall. I was really impressed by his mien... I had thought that he would be dressed in a khadi kurta, dhoti, chappals, and have a fountain pen. And there he was, a real saheb. I was hesitant to ask him to stay in the small house that I had...

Although he was a slim and frail person, he was very active and alert. He was a clever speaker and would speak one sentence in English and another one in Hindi. 'I was keen to have your darshan,' he said, 'and you are exactly what I had imagined you to be. Today I feel my own true identity. For until now I was only a prisoner.'

'Have you resigned from the job?' I asked.

'No', he said, 'I have taken leave. I haven't even received my salary for the month. I told them to send it to me at your address... It is a good job...but I have to work very hard, and I get hardly any time for literary pursuits.'

That night, I made him sleep in my room. The next day I fixed up a hotel for him. The hotel management expected some advance payment. Joshi had none. I had to pay Rs 30. I thought his monthly salary would be received soon and the advance given would be reimbursed.

I have a friend whose name is Mathur. I had told him about Joshi. When he learnt that Joshi was there, he rushed to the hotel to meet him. The two became good friends. Joshi would now visit me twice or thrice a day and once late in the evening. He was a jack of all trades, a connoisseur of music, a good harmonium player and clever with magical tricks. He cooked well too.

A month passed. Joshi's salary did not reach him. I did not mention this subject lest he should think that I was demanding the money advanced to the hotel.

Joshi started visiting Mathur regularly. Whenever Joshi came over to see me he always talked of Mathur and when Mathur visited he praised Joshi. Joshi had a fund of interesting experiences. He had been in the army. When his fiancè married another man he left the army. And whenever he referred to his parents, his uncle or aunt, his eyes would fill with tears. One day, Joshi spoke highly of his own play. It was staged in Calcutta, he said, and the manager of Madan Theatres had congratulated him. Joshi read out three or four extracts from the play. I liked it very much. He said he had sold it to a publisher in Kashi for just Rs 20. I told him to get the play back, and that I would pay him the Rs 20. 'This play is good,' I told him. 'It should be given to a publisher of repute or get staged by a good theatrical company.'

Four days later, he told me that the publisher would return it only if he were paid Rs 50 because, he said, a part of it had already been printed. I told him to get the play back, even if we had to pay Rs 50. The play was received by VPP and I paid Rs 50.

It was almost month since Joshi had come. The hotel was to ask again for advance payment for the next month. I was feeling quite concerned. Then Joshi told me that he was shifting to Mathur's house.

'He is a poor man,' he said, 'and if I pay him Rs 20 a month he will be able to pull along.' I felt relieved and happy. The next day Joshi shifted to Mathur's house.

Whenever Joshi came to me, he brought some news about Mathur. I was aware that Mathur's financial position was not a happy one. The poor fellow had held a job in the railways. His services were terminated. But I did not know that he was on the verge of starvation, or that his landlord had come and rebuked him, or that his milkman, grocer and clothier had also done the same. He could not show his face to his creditors. Joshi narrated Mathur's tale of woe. And when he told me all this, he had tears in his eyes. I had thought that I was the only person in distress. Hearing Mathur's tale of woes, I forgot my own troubles.

'You are only worried about yourself and are not concerned with Mathur's troublés,' I told myself. 'If I go to any friend's house, I would certainly get food. There is poor Mathur with his mother, two widowed older sisters, one niece, two nephews and one younger brother. For such a large family, Rs 50 a month was too little for their basic needs. Mathur is truly a very brave man, bearing the burden of a large family courageously. He is an angel. And now Joshi was not worrying about himself but was worried about Mathur.'

One day Joshi came and said to me. 'At last I have found a way out for Mathur... I have a friend, a bar-at-law, also named Mathur.

I am negotiating with him for the marriage of our common friend Mathur's niece Jaggo. I will arrange to send one of Mathur's widowed sisters and her children away with the niece to her in-laws. The widowed sister is agreeable to shift to her husband's younger brother's house. When this is through, Mathur will only have three or four people to be looked after. I'll contribute something. Mathur too will earn something. Today the landlord has to be paid two months' rent. He had parked himself opposite the house this morning, and says that he will go only after receiving the rent. If you could spare just Rs 30, please give it to me. Mathur's younger brother would be getting his month's salary in a day or two. Our friend was in dire need, and friend was recommending his case. I did not have the heart to say no.

Despite the disapproval of my wife, I gave the money. Having given the money, it occurred to me that Mathur is always in trouble. How long would I be able to bail him out?

Joshi was to get him a job. It was a coincidence that a friend from Agra came to meet me. He was a member of the Legislative Council. He had written plays and was fond of music. He knew many wealthy people. He was romantically inclined too. When he visited me, I mentioned the case of Joshi and read out extracts from his play. 'Send him with me,' he said. 'I will appoint him as my private secretary. He can stay in my house as a member of my family. He will get Rs 30 a month as pocket money. He will help me write plays.'

I was happy and told Joshi. He was ready to go but, he said, he needed some money before he could go. For, he said, he could not if poorly dressed, accompany a gentleman. And it would not be appropriate to ask him for money on the first day. After deleting all the unnecessary items, a few items were considered absolutely necessary, and these would cost at least Rs 40. I did not have the money and could not muster the courage to ask my wife...

Arrangements would have to be made. After Joshi got the money, he dressed well and was able to accompany the legislator. I went to the railway station to see him off. So did Mathur. When I returned, I felt a great burden off me.

'He is a very affectionate person,' said Mathur.

'He is like a brother to me,' I said.

'Without him my home will not be the same again,' said Mathur. 'Everyone at home wept; he did not behave like an outsider... He talked to my mother like another son, and to my sister like a brother would.'

'He is an unfortunate fellow,' I said. 'Otherwise why should he, the son of a father earning more than Rs 2000 a month, be running from pillar to post... His father owns two houses in Darjeeling.'

'Joshi wants to take me there,' said Mathur. 'And he will certainly go back in a year or two. When he goes there, he tells me, he would get me an agency for motor cars.'

Both of us returned home, building castles in the air.

I felt very happy that at last Joshi had got an opening. I hoped that now that Joshi would be getting a salary, he would return to me what he owed me. He would perhaps take four or five months to pay me, for the amount he owed me seemed quite sizeable when calculated.

'All that has happened,' I said to myself, 'has been good for me. For, I could not have saved this amount otherwise.' It also occurred to me that I should ask my friend to give me some money every month, to be adjusted against his salary.

Before the end of one month, I saw Joshi and Mathur coming towards me together. I wondered whether Joshi had given up this job too. Laying aside my apprehensions, I asked Joshi, 'When did you come? And how are you?'

Joshi sat down, lit his cigar and said, 'I am very well indeed.

My boss is a thorough gentleman. He has given me a room all to myself. He makes me dine with him and treats me like a brother. He has gone to Delhi. And rather than getting bored I told myself that I should come here and meet you.' He added, 'Before he left for Delhi, the boss asked me to buy some utensils from Muradabad for him. But he forgot to give me the money for these wares. I thought it would not be correct for me to ask him for money. Please give me Rs 50. Within two days of my journey back, I will remit it to you. Of course, you know how correct the boss is in regard to money matters.'

I did not like this request at all. But then it concerned my friend who had been very kind to me. At that time I had Rs 50 with which I was to buy paper for my magazine. I gave this to Joshi. That evening, Mathur came to me and told me that Joshi had already gone because he had got a telegram from his boss.

'Joshi,' said Mathur, 'is a really large-hearted man. He behaves like one of us. He is childlike in so many ways. He told me he was arranging my niece's marriage. There would be no dowry. However, some expenses would have to be incurred on presents. The barrister-in-law whom she will wed stays in Delhi and we will have to take some presents when we go there. Joshi will go there, and I have given him some money for this reason. It will be a great burden off my head.'

'But you did not have the money to give,' I said to Mathur.

'I did not have it,' said Mathur, 'I took it from the mahajan at 2 per cent monthly interest. I had to sign a stamped receipt for it.'

Another two months passed. Joshi visited me twice or thrice. He did not ask me for more money and talked a lot about his boss which provided me with material for a few short stories.

The following May, Joshi arrived suddenly one day. He told me that his boss had gone to Nainital. The boss had asked him to accompany him, he said, but Joshi would rather be with us and hence came here. Then Joshi narrated some incidents. One day, he said, he had gone to the bank of the Jamuna for a stroll. 'There was to be a swimming contest. Lots of spectators had gathered. I also stood there, watching the show. Not far from me stood a gentleman and a young woman. When I started conversing with them, I learnt that they belonged to my community and also that they knew my father and uncle. They talked to me affectionately.

"Why are you running from pillar to post?" they asked. "You should go back to your parents. Their behaviour towards you might not have been model but surely the parents have a right over their children and your mother must be feeling miserable."' He added, 'A young man came along and said to the old man and the young woman I was talking to, "Don't you feel ashamed that you and the young daughter are standing like this in the fair." The old man felt embarrassed and the woman put on her veil and stepped back. It now became known that the young man was to marry the woman. The old man was a large-hearted and enlightened person. He did not believe in the practice of purdah. The young man, despite his age, was extremely conservative, and a great advocate of purdah. The old man continued talking like an accused on the defensive, but the young man was aggressive. Then the old man also became firm and adopted an aggressive posture. The young man retorted. "I consider the proposal to marry this daughter of yours a disgrace."

'The old man was really furious. He said, "I consider it a shameful act to marry my daughter to a dissolute fellow like you." In his anger the young man, caught hold of the old man and pushed him. Vanquished in argument, he now came to use force. The old man fell down. I rushed forward to help him get up, and challenged the young man. The young man struggled with me. I am no wrestler but the young man knew the art of wrestling. In a few moments he dropped me and caught hold of my throat.

Several people collected there. People were enjoying the spectacle of the two of us grappling with each other. When, however, they saw the situation taking a turn for the worse, they advanced and disengaged us. The young man, while leaving, said to the old man, "If you exhibit your daughter like a prostitute, you may do what you wish to, but I will not marry her." The old man was stunned and the young woman was crying.'

Joshi said, 'I could not stand all this, and told the old man, "You are like my father, and you know me. If you consider me to be a suitable match for your daughter, I would consider myself lucky to make your daughter the mistress of my heart. You see the state I am in. Maybe I'll pass the rest of my days like this. However, if devotion, service and love can make life happy, then I firmly believe that I will not be wanting in doing all these for the young lady." The old man was overjoyed and hugged me. He took me to his house, hosted a dinner and gave me a customary gift as a token of matrimony. I was keen to meet the young lady to ascertain her willingness. The old man gladly permitted me to do so. After meeting the girl I saw that she was a gem of a person. I was surprised at her comprehension. She fitted into the image I had conjectured for my life partner.

'I know that my life with her would be a happy one. "Please bless me, I told the old man."' Joshi continued, 'It has now been agreed that the marriage would be solemnized in June. I told them that the clothes and ornaments that I would provide would be the minimum and there should be no pomp. When I told the old man about you, and that you were like my parent, he was very happy. He reads your articles with great interest and respect.'

A bit upset, I told Joshi that he was in no position to get married. If nothing else, he should at least have some regular income, at least Rs 50 a month.

Said Joshi, 'If I get married, I will lead a normal life. The reason why I left my home was on the issue of marriage, and the reason for my return home would also be my marriage. When Promilla, with folded hands, falls at the feet of my father, his stony heart will melt. When the marriage has already been solemnized, he will say, "Why torture this poor bride". And when she is welcomed by them, they will call me back on their own. I had left home because I was adamant that I would marry without any dowry and now that my vow will be fulfilled, I will go back. Promilla is really a very sensible person. She will win over my people. And my marriage, I have estimated, would entail a total expenditure of Rs 300. I would get some Rs 3000–4000 from my in-laws. I have thought it all over. I will first bring Promilla here. And it is from here that she would write to my people. After three days, you will see, my uncle will come here with a box of jewellery. After I get married, they can't do a thing about it. That is why I haven't sent them any confirmation.'

'I have no money,' I said, 'Where will you get Rs 300 from?'

'It won't be Rs 300 cash down,' said Joshi. 'Rs 100 for clothes, another Rs 100 for customary basic items and Rs 100 for the journey. The bride's house is in Kashipur and the marriage will be solemnized there. The Bengali goldsmith opposite your house will, on your order, give the ornaments I ask for within a week. So will the clothier. Rs 100 will be all the cash that will be needed. And this amount I will pay back as soon as I return. The wedding party will consist of me, you and Mathur. I don't wish to bother you. As you have been helpful and treated me like a brother, please help me just once more. I am confident that you will not object to the fulfillment of this auspicious work. It is only because of this confidence in you that I have given my word of honour.'

So Joshi laid the burden of clothes worth Rs 100 on me, ornaments worth another Rs 100 and money for the journey was to be borrowed from a friend. Joshi was joined by some friends. There was some merriment at the time of the marriage. The bride's father looked after the guests conscientiously. He had to rush to join work and left the following day. But Mathur kept Joshi company until the end of the formalities. Then Mathur also returned, empty-handed. Nothing was given by Joshi's in-laws. Mathur came to know that the story of Joshi meeting with the girl and the father-in-law on the banks of the Jamuna was false and also that Joshi had been in regular correspondence with the girl for quite some time. So was the story of Joshi fixing up a husband for Mathur's niece. The story of rent being paid to Mathur's landlord and its being borrowed was also a lie. Mathur said that Joshi was dishonest, had not given him the money to be paid as house rent, nor any money for food. 'In fact,' he said, 'he had taken Rs 100 from the mahajan in my name and I had given a proper receipt. I did not know he was cheating me all this time.'

As if by coincidence, my friend from Agra with whom he had stayed for some time, arrived. Seeing Mathur, he said, 'I see that you are still alive. Joshi told me that you were dead.' Said Mathur, 'Dead! I did not have even a headache.' And did you receive those brass utensils which you had asked him to buy from Muradabad?' I asked.

'Which utensils from Muradabad?' asked my Agra-based friend.

'Which you asked Joshi to buy.'

'I never asked Joshi for anything. If I had wanted anything I would have written to you myself.'

'So he gobbled up that money too,' said Mathur.

Said the Agra-based friend, 'He had taken Rs 100 from me on the pretext of your funeral ceremonies. He is really a great cheat.'

'What frauds he has committed. It is the first time in my life that I have been cheated like this. I'll get him sentenced to imprisonment for at least three years. Anyhow, where is he these days.'

'He is at his in-laws,' said Mathur.

'Yes, Joshi had cheated everyone he knew, even a poor and good man like Mathur and the clever Agra-based gentleman. If he had not been exposed, he would have many more people.'

'Be that as it may,' I said. 'I was deeply impressed by the clever ways of this cheat. He is a master-mind.'

...And then, the police arrived in search of this cheat, who was a fugitive from law and an absconder.

And what did my wife think of me? Here is what she thought.

SIXTEEN

A LARGE PART OF MY LIFE HAS BEEN SPENT IN MY HUSBAND'S house but I have never had peace. In the eyes of the world, my husband is a thorough gentleman, a civil, cultured, large-hearted and charming person. However, only the wife knows what he is, because she experiences it. The world takes delight in praising those who ignore their own interest and expend all that they have on others. They do not praise those who do something for their own families. For such men are, according to them, selfish, miserly and narrow-minded. Likewise, why should those in the house praise those who do all they can for outsiders only? Look at my husband. He troubles me a lot. I don't observe purdah. I don't like going to the market for groceries. And when he is asked to shop, he goes to shops that no one else patronizes. In such shops, you neither get stuff of good quality, nor is the weight accurate, nor is the price proper. For if it was, why would that shop not be popular? And yet, such are the shops that my husband always patronizes. I have told him many times that he should always buy from shops that are popular because their stocks get sold out quickly. But no, he prefers worthless shopkeepers and they all cheat him. The wheat he gets is of the worst quality available, the rice is rotten and so coarse that even bullocks won't eat it, and lentil, which is full of pebbles, burns any amount of firewood, yet will not cook. The ghee he gets is half oil. Its weight too, it would be at least one-sixteenth less. And the hair oil he gets is certainly adulterated; when it is applied to the hair, the hair sticks. And he pays for pure amla oil. It seems to me that he is afraid of entering a shop that is frequented by too many people, believing that the bigger the shop, the poorer is the stuff available there. In my experience, you get inferior stuff in shops that are not popular.

If one experiences this once, one could perhaps bear with it. But not when it is repeated day after day it becomes irksome. I ask my husband why he goes only to third-rate shops. 'Or have you taken it upon yourself to ensure that they survive? When they see you, they invite you into the shops. It sounds wonderful. They beckon you, talk to you sweetly and lavish praise on you. They make you feel on top of the world.

My husband is indifferent to the packaging of useless stuff. When I ask him why he should go only to these cheats and not to others and why he is so sweet to them, he has no answer. And silence defeats a hundred arguments. Once I asked him to get me an ornament.

'Goldsmiths,' he said, 'are never to be trusted. You will get cheated. I know a goldsmith who was my classmate. We played games together for years. He won't cheat me.'

I said to myself, 'If he is his childhood friend, he'll play fair.' I therefore trusted him and gave my husband one ornament for exchange and Rs 100 in cash. I don't know to whom my esteemed husband gave the ornament and the cash. After an anxious wait for the new ornament, I did get it at last. It had 50 per cent copper and it was so ugly that I hated looking at it. I felt that my aspirations for years had gone in vain. I cried myself hoarse and cursed the goldsmith. In any case, I know his friends are not really so trustworthy and would not hesitate to cut the throats of their friends. And I do think that, by and large, his friends are known cheats, pickpockets, vagabonds and scoundrels, whose only profession is to make friends with those who behave like blind men. Almost everyday, I find that there is someone who comes to him to borrow money and won't leave until he has succeeded in achieving his objective. And I don't remember a single occasion when the debtor has paid back the money borrowed from my husband. Having been cheated once, one becomes careful, and more so when one is cheated a second time. However, here is a man who has been cheated a thousand times and has not yet learnt his lesson. When I ask him why he does not ask the person to whom he has loaned money to repay it, or ask if that friend is no longer alive, he evades the issue. For, he cannot say 'no' to his friends. I tell him, don't say 'no', but you can give one excuse or another. My husband is keen that the world thinks he is prosperous. Indeed, his keenness is such that in order to ensure that the world thinks that he is really well off, he would even mortgage my ornaments to oblige them.

There have been occasions when I have been absolutely broke. And here is my noble husband who almost hates to see money in the house. Until the time he spends all there is in the house, he won't have his peace of mind.

How much can I describe his misdoings? I am really fed up. Every day he brings along one guest or another, and they all come like messengers of death. I don't know where his vagrant friends come from. Some come from here, some from there and some from nowhere. My house seems to be a refuge for the handicapped.

The house in which we live is small. In my room there is space for only two beds and there is no place for a third bed. And yet, here is this great husband of mine who extends invitations to friends. If he is to be in his room, his friend also must have a bed there too. In summer, accommodating these people does not matter because there is the terrace we can use for guests, while I and the children live as if in a cage. But in winter...only God knows...

My husband does not understand that things being what they are, he should not invite those who come without proper clothing and, God be praised, most of his friends belong to this category. He is oblivious to the effect these exposures have on the children. Among his friends, there is not a single one who in time of dire need would give him even token assistance. Once or twice, he did undergo extremely bitter experiences, but then he is a person who seems to have taken an oath to stay blind. Such are the people with whom he gets on well. There are lots of people whom the goddess of wealth has bestowed her favours on, but he does not know even one of them. His pride stops him from going to meet them. He will befriend only those who have no place of their own.

I recall once, our water-carrier had left. For several days, we did not have another one. I was in search of an efficient one and could wait. But my husband was obsessed with the idea of engaging one immediately. The work in the household was as usual, but he felt there was some dislocation. My washing dishes and his going to the bazaar for groceries was unbearable to him. A man, Ghuray, wild and uncouth, was described by my husband in glowing terms. Ghuray according to my husband, was clever, very obedient, extremely hard working, well-mannered and very honest. I engaged him.

That I accept whatever he says, is really a surprise to me. This newcomer had only the appearance of a human being, but there were no other signs of his being one. He did not have even rudimentary sense. He was not dishonest but was an absolute ass. Had he been dishonest, the saving grace would have been that at least he was helping himself. The unfortunate fellow was cheated by shopkeepers too. He did not know how to count even upto ten. If I sent him to the bazaar with a rupee in the morning, he was unable to explain how he had spent it in the evening. I naturally sulked. I was livid with anger and I wished to pull his ears. But I never saw my husband say anything to him. Far be it from him to pull him up. When my husband had a bath and was washing his dhoti, this odd creature was watching listlessly from some distance. If I had been in my husband's position, I would have ingested him. But my husband did not bother. If my taunts had made the odd man help with washing the dhoti, he would not have been allowed even to approach him. My husband praised the man and made his deficiencies virtues! He would hide his defects.

This fool did not know how to sweep the floors. The living room was the only worthwhile room in the house. When he swept this room, he would place some items on the wrong side and others upside down. It would appear as if the room had been hit by an earthquake. Beside, there was so much dust floating in the air, it was difficult to breathe. And there would be my dear husband sitting absolutely calm and peaceful. Then one day, I gave Ghuray a warning that if from the following day he did not sweep properly, I would turn him out. Next morning, when I woke up, I found the room in good shape, each item in its proper place. There was not a speck of dust anywhere. When I appeared surprised, my husband smiled and said, 'Ghuray has swept the room quite early this morning. This is because I have explained to him how it is to be done. That is the way of doing it. You don't give him instructions, you only taunt him. I was happy and thanked God that at last Ghuray had done something which was in order and that in future the room would be properly swept. Ghuray, in my eyes, now seemed like a person who could sweep properly.

Then by chance, I got up quite early one morning. Ghuray was standing at the door, and my husband was sweeping the room zealously. I was really angry, my eyes were bloodshot. I snatched the broom from my husband's hands and struck it on Ghuray's head. I sacked him on the spot.

'Please pay him a month's salary,' said my husband.

'What for?' I asked. 'Do no work, show your anger and get your full wages!' I did not pay him even one penny. I had already given him a shirt. I snatched it from him. For several days, my husband was cross with me. One day, he was about to leave the house when he was stopped with great difficulty. 'The world is full of such fools,' I said to myself. 'Had I not been there, someone might have even sold him off as a commodity by now.'

Then another day our scavenger asked for old clothes. Now these days, none except a policeman or a rich man has old clothes to spare. Let alone old clothes in my house, there are never any spare clothes. My husband's entire wardrobe would fit into a small attache case that can be sent by post. And we cannot afford woollen clothes for winter. When there is no money, how could one have clothes? I told the scavenger the position. I had also felt that this winter was very cold. And I knew what it would mean to poor people. But my husband and I had nothing to give, except our regrets. As long as the present social system exists, such complaints would raise their heads. If wealthy men have coachfuls of clothes in the winter, poor people would have to go about virtually naked. I told the scavenger to go. But do you know what my husband did? He took off his coat and gave it to him. I was shocked and incensed. I am not so charity minded as to feed others and go to sleep hungry. Shrimanji, my husband, had only one coat. He did not bother to think about what he would put on. It seems to me that his lust for fame had dulled his senses. The scavenger thanked him, prayed for his long life and was gone. My husband shivered for a few days. He gave up his morning walks. God has indeed given him a heart. He is not at all bothered about putting on old, worn-out or tattered clothes. I feel ashamed to see him wearing these. If someone makes fun of him on this account, he says, 'Let him do so.' When I could not bear his not having a warm coat, I got him one. I was so cut up with him for his action that I felt like allowing him to shiver. But I thought he might fall sick. That would be worse. It is he who has to work and earn the bread.

My husband must think he is benevolent and how noble the deed was. He may indeed be proud of such acts. But I do not think such deeds are noble or benevolent or humane. It is just stupid and callous indifference. I had seen this scavenger dead drunk sometimes. And I had also pointed it out to my husband. The question was whether we should be indifferent and ignore their weaknesses and foolishness.

If you are really compassionate and kind, I say, you should be large-hearted towards your own people also. Or is this large-heartedness reserved for outsiders only, and your own kith and kin are to be denied its largesse.

I have spent so many years of my life with my husband but he has never given me a present. I must admit, however, that whenever I have asked him to get me something he has never objected, provided, of course, that I give him the money for it. He is never keen to buy and, in fact, never buys himself anything. He is quite content with whatever I buy for him. Every man, at least sometimes, wishes to buy things of his own choice, but not my husband. I see lots of people buy ornaments for their wives, buy different dresses, or cosmetics. But here, in this house, there is a complete ban on such items. In his life he has never bought sweets, toys or musical instruments for the children. He seems to have taken a vow in this regard. I would therefore say that he is a miser and an unromantic, heartless being.

His idea of service to others is aimed only at getting fame and a semblance of indifference to the ways of the world. As for his humility, he has never been social with any official in his life. To salute his senior officers is against his principles. Far be it from him to give a nazar, gifts or daali. He never calls on any officer at his house. If he were not to suffer the consequences for such behaviour who else would? While others get special leave, he has a cut effected in his salary. Others get promotions, but no one thinks of his promotion. If he is late by five minutes, an explanation is expected. He works very hard and if there is an onerous or difficult job to be done, he is entrusted it. His colleagues in the office all him Ghissu Pissu, a penpusher. This refers to his hard-working nature. Hard work he may be entrusted with, but his luck does not get him any reward or recognition. His humility and his independent outlook, are perhaps a mark of his inefficiency and apathy towards the ways of the world. Why should your boss be happy with you, only because you are hardworking.

Affairs of the world are guided by a code and traditions. If you are indifferent to these, there is no reason why your counterpart should also be indifferent. If feelings in your heart are strong, it would be apparent in your behaviour in the office. If one tries to please the boss or takes any action that benefits the boss personally, the boss would favour him. Also, why should others have sympathy with people like my husband? The boss is a human being. How would the boss's wish be respected and held in esteem by the subordinates? If the subordinates don't give him respect, would the boss come to salute them? The result has been that my husband has never worked in the same office for more than two or three years. Wherever he has worked, his services were terminated. Either he quarrelled with the bosses or he left because there was too much work.

He claims sometimes that he looks after a large family – several cousins and their children – and that he is always keen to know their wants, and this while none of them care for him in the least. One of his cousins is a tehsildar these days, but the responsibility of looking after his family is my husband's. The tehsildar lives in great style, maintains a car and has many servants to attend on him. But he has left his family to be looked after by his cousin. He never even writes a letter.

Once we were short of money and I asked my husband why should he not write a letter to his cousin. 'Why should I bother him,' he said. 'He has to live his own life too. And how much can he save.' When I insisted that he write, he did send a letter. I don't know what he wrote in the letter, or whether or not he actually wrote it or merely pretended. No money was received. Nor was the receipt of the letter acknowledged. Several days later, I asked my husband whether there was a response from the court of his dear brother. He retorted furiously. 'It is only a week since the letter had reached him. How can he reply so soon?' Another week passed and yet there was no reply. He does not give me an opportunity to refer to the issue. But he appears to be happy and carefree, returns home smiling, and refers to some other subjects. He flatters me. My parents' names are now referred to, accompanied with lavish praise. My management of the home affairs is also appreciated – I think all these praises are lavished so that I don't question him about his brother's reply to the letter. Various political, economic and social issues and a code of conduct come up for discussion and are all expounded upon at such great lengths that even experts would throw in the towel. And all this to ensure that I do not ask questions on this one topic.

But I am not one to give in so easily. After two weeks, when the deadline for the insurance premium arrived and reminders came like the summons of death, I asked him – 'Has your dear brother sent you a message or is it that your letter did not reach him? We also have a share in the ancestral property, don't we? Or are you the progeny of a domestic maid.'

Ten years ago, the ancestral estate yielded an income of Rs 5000 a year. It should now be more than Rs 10,000. But we don't get even one penny. Roughly speaking, we should be getting at least 2000. If not 2000, at least 1000, or even 500, or 250, in others words, something to pay at least the insurance premium with. The tehsildar saheb earns at least four times what you earn. He takes bribes too, why doesn't he pay us something at least?

My husband tried to evade the issue by saying 'hay hay' or 'haan haan' or 'That poor fellow has had the house repaired, he plays host to all the relations and spends on gifts for them. Where then are his means to enable him to send us any money.'

His understanding of the situation is inept. He thinks the ancestral property is there to earn rent to carry out repairs only. This man does not know how to make excuses or to spin yarns. Had he asked me, I would have told him a few, not just one, but thousands of them and one better than the other. He could have said the house was burnt down or that there was a theft in the house and nothing was left behind, or that stocks of Rs 10,000 worth of foodgrains had been damaged, that there was a fight and a subsequent criminal case leading to bankruptcy. However, whatever he could think of as an excuse was worthless and meaningless. I cursed my bad luck. I had to borrow from a neighbour to meet our immediate needs. He praises his cousins and their progeny to the skies. Whenever I hear these praises I get livid. God save us from such relations, from such descendants of the Kauravas (of the *Mahabharata*). By the grace of God, we have two sons and two daughters. Be it His Grace or His curse, all four children are extremely diligent. But my husband can never be stern. The other day, the elder son went out and had not returned till 8 o'clock. I was in a panic. But my husband was cool. He sat reading his newspaper. Annoyed, I advanced towards him, snatched the paper and said to him, 'Why don't you go and see where the boy is. You don't care at all. I don't really know why God has given you these children. A father should take an interest in his son.'

My husband reacted. 'Has he not returned home yet? he said. 'He is a devil. When he returns tonight, I will pull his ears... No, I will flog him so hard that his skin will come off.' And then, in this temper and bad mood, he set out in search of the boy. It was just a coincidence that soon after he went out, the boy turned up and entered the house. I asked him where had had come from. He did not reply. I told him, 'Your father has gone out in search of you. He was gnashing his teeth in anger. You will have to face the music today. He is about to return. He has a stick in his hands. You have become stubborn these days and don't listen to anybody. Today you will know what's what.'

Fear gripped the boy. He lit the lamp and sat down to study. My husband returned in about two hours. He was in an intemperate mood. Entering the house, he first asked, 'Has he returned yet or not?' To precipitate matters, I told him, 'Here he is, why don't you ask him yourself? I have given up asking him where he had gone. He does not reply.'

'Mannu, come here,' thundered my husband. The boy, shivering in fear, came forward and stood in the courtyard. The two girls hid themselves, afraid something terrible should happen. The younger brother was peeping like a rat through the window.

My husband was agitated. He had a stick in his hand. Seeing him so angry I regretted that I had complained to him. He went to the boy, but instead of hitting him with the stick, he placed his hand on his shoulders and, in a mere show of anger, asked him where he had gone. 'You have been told not to go out like this, but you don't do as you are told. I am warning you not to be so late. You should be at home, not loitering about.'

I thought this was only the preamble, and that the real thing will follow. The preamble was certainly not bad, but then it ended with the preamble only. Like the pre-monsoon gathering of dark clouds, his anger was akin to some thunder and then a little drizzle. The boy went to his room and was dancing joyfully.

I told my husband, 'You seem to have retracted. You should have at least given him a few slaps. The way you handle them, will make them bold.'

Do you know what my husband said to me? 'Did not you hear how I rebuked him,' he said. 'The boy must have been terrified. He will never be late again.'

'You did not rebuke him,' I said, 'you only wiped his tears.'

He said, 'Didn't you really hear my rebuke to him?'

'Yes,' I said, 'and what a rebuke it was. Nobody's ears heard it. Come, let me massage your throat.'

My husband has developed a new strategy. According to this, boys, when punished, become bad. Instead of punishing them they should be made to feel free. And they should not be subjected to any pressure, discipline or any sort, on curbs. Discipline hampers the process of the child's growth and development. That's why boys now behave like camels without the nose strings. They don't spend time in reading books, they play gulli–danda, or marbles, or fly kites...

Incidentally, my husband sometimes joins them in their games. He is now forty years old, yet he behaves like a child. No one dared play gulli–danda or fly kites before my father. He would have finished them. He would sit down with them in the mornings so that they studied. In the evenings, after they returned from school, he would make them sit down again. He would give them only half an hour off at dusk time. At night too, he would yoke them. He himself was not reading the newspaper and allowing the children to loiter about in the street. And my husband?… he sometimes behaves like a calf shorn of its horns. He sits down with them to play a game of cards. How can people like him set an example to their boys. My own brother dared not look into the eyes of father. Whenever we heard our father's voice, there would be commotion in the house. Once he had entered the house, there was the rule of silence. The boys were afraid to approach him. It was because of his stern discipline that the boys have done well and reached high positions. Of course, their health, I admit, is not too good. But then my father's own health was also not very good. He was always on drugs or medicines.

Anyway, what happened one day was unusual. My husband was giving instructions to the children on how to fly a kite, how to pull it and how to let it go, how to make it change direction, etc. He was in fact teaching them with great zeal, as if he was instructing them in guru mantra. That day, I really took him to task to teach him a lesson he would not forget.

'Why the hell,' I said, 'are you spoiling my children? You may not be concerned with household affairs, but please don't spoil my children, don't teach them bad ways. You have failed to change me, but don't spoil them.'

My husband averted his head.

Sometimes I feel that he should really get provoked, so that I can react and show him my face of a witch. But he yields so easily and coolly that I feel like I have been defeated.

My father never allowed the children to go to any fair or entertainment shows. The boys would get desperate but my father would not be moved. And here, on the other hand, is my husband who beckons the sons to go to the fair, telling them, 'Come on boys, let us go, there is great fun there, fireworks, balloons, a foreign merry-go-round. You will get a good ride. What's more, there is no one to stop you from playing hockey.' I think foreign games, e.g., cricket, football and hockey are all nearly fatal, one more than the other. If a ball hits you, it might mean the end of you. And yet, my husband is fond of all these games. When one of the boys wins a game and comes to him, he feels so elated, as if the boy has conquered a fort. He is least bothered about what might happen, even severe injury.

Our daughter was to get married. He was dead set that not a penny was to be given as dowry, even if the daughter was to remain unmarried for her whole life. Such was his idealism. He is aware of the devious ways prevalent in our society, but has kept his eyes averted. So long as the present social system remains unchanged and it is a matter of shame for a girl to stay unmarried, the present state of affairs will continue. There may be a few exceptions when the bridegroom's people do not stretch out their hands but these exceptions do not change the situation.

My husband can deliver sermons against the dowry system and yet I have not come across one person who turns down an offer of dowry. This present system will change if the facilities offered to the girls for education and livelihood are the same as those for the boys. Whenever I negotiated about my daughter's marriage, the question of dowry came up, and on each occasion it became a stumbling block. When a whole year passed and the girl entered her seventeenth year, I arranged a groom. He agreed because the bridegroom's side did not raise the question of dowry. They did not raise it perhaps because they knew that a hefty sum would be given anyway. I had decided that I would leave no stone unturned to see that this goes smoothly. There were still doubts about whether matters would go smoothly. But I succeeded in my efforts and made my husband agree to the marriage. He continued to say that this system of ours was shameful and meaningless.

'Why should there be any expenditure in a marriage? Why must you arrange a musical soiree?' He said I had disgraced his name. Just imagine all these arguments when the bridegroom's party was at the threshold of the house. The auspicious moment for the solemn event was past midnight. As per the custom I observed a fast, even though he continued to insist that there was no need for a fast. 'When the bridegroom or his people do not observe a fast,' he said, 'why should those of the bride keep a fast.'

Other members of my family and I impressed upon him to observe a fast. But he had his breakfast and his lunch too. Anyhow, the time for giving our daughter's hand came. He had always been opposed to this system of gifting away the daughter along with the dowry. A daughter, he says, is not a commodity to be gifted away in daan. 'You can gift land, money or animals but to gift away a daughter is really mean,' he said. I have told him many times that this practice is very ancient and goes back to the time of the Vedas, that it is mentioned in all the sacred texts. All the relatives tell him this is so. The priests also tell him it is so. But he remains untouched. I entreat him, I fall at his feet and beg of him, but he refuses to enter the mandap. He not only behaved badly, but was also annoyed with me. For several months after my daughter's wedding, he did not speak to me. I had to yield to bring him around.

The greatest irony of the situation is that despite all his weaknesses I cannot remain without him even for a moment. Yes, despite all his faults, I am deeply in love with him. I don't really know why. There is something in him which makes me his slave. If he is a little late in returning home, I am on tenterhooks. If God were to send someone in his place, someone who is the epitome of knowledge and wisdom or a man of great wealth or good looks, I wouldn't look at him. It isn't just because of a religious duty or the oath of fidelity that binds me to him.

There has been a growth or development between the two of us, like two parts of a machine that get ground so much that they fit each other perfectly. On the road we have travelled together and are familiar with, we can march ahead unhesitatingly with our eyes closed, even though all the turnings and twists, ups and downs might be hidden. And how bothersome it could be to walk on an untreaded path...

I won't be willing to exchange his defects for virtues.

* * *

Despite our differences in approach in domestic matters, we shared views in national matters.

On the political front, anomalies by the government had become unbearable. The behaviour of the police towards Pundit Jawaharlal Nehru's mother was so unbearable that it was almost shameful to be out of jail.

My wife was arrested while picketing a shop selling foreign cloth. She was sentenced to two months' imprisonment. I saw her in jail and found her cheerful as ever. I wanted to go to jail but she blocked my way. I have fallen down in my own esteem, she has gone up a hundredfold...

My writings have offended the government several times. One or two of my books were proscribed. I have never been to jail. I am not a man of action.

Lucknow had become a military camp. The army was all over. The police and British soldiers were camping in both the parks of Aminabad. Section 144 was enforced. The Congress was keen to defy it. The police were arresting people.

SEVENTEEN

THERE WAS EXCITEMENT IN THE VILLAGES. THE MUD HUTS seemed full of smiles. A batch of satyagrahis was to come to the village. A pandal had been erected in front of Kodai Chaudhri's house to receive them. Flour, ghee, vegetables, milk and curd were collected. On everybody's face there was hope, determination and joy.

The same Binda Ahir who used to hide for fear of having to supply a quarter-seer of milk free to officers on tour, had today collected, of his own accord, two huge earthen pitchers full of milk and curd from the cow-house and had brought them there. The potter, who similarly used to run away from home, had today brought a pile of pitchers. The barbers and water-carriers also ran to the scene – and this of their own accord. If there was anyone sad in the village today, it was the old woman Nohri who sat at the entrance of her hut and watched all these preparations with her seventy-five-year-old sunken eyes. She had regrets. For what could she take to Kodai's door and say, 'I have brought this as my offering?' Today, she had to look to others for even her food.

Nohri had seen better days. There was a time when she had wealth, a family and everything else. She had virtually ruled the village and had kept Kodai under check. Though a woman, she was as good as a man. While her husband would sleep at home, she would keep watch in the fields. She would pursue even law suits, and collect all her dues. But fate had now snatched away everything from her. She had neither the riches, nor the big family. She had remained behind as if to mourn them all. Her eyes couldn't see and her ears couldn't hear. It was difficult for her even to move about. Somehow or the other, she was passing her last days.

On the other hand, fortune had smiled on Kodai. He was now sought after everywhere, and he had access to everyone. Even today's celebration was being held at his doorstep. 'Who would care for Nohri?' As she thought about this, her heart was trampled as if it were under a heavy boulder. Had God not crippled her to this extent, she would certainly have pasted her hut with cowdung, had a band at her doorstep and treated everyone to a feast of halwa and poorees. And after the people had feasted, she would have presented them with a handful of coins.

She did remember the day when she had taken her old husband and travelled more than twenty miles just to have a glimpse of the Mahatma (Gandhi). Enthusiasm, pure devotion and reverence surged up in her heart now – like dark clouds.

Kodai came up to her. 'Mahatmaji's procession will be here today, my sister-in-law,' he said with his toothless mouth. 'Would you too give something?'

Nohri looked at Kodai Chaudhri piercingly. 'The cruel man has come to torture me. He wants to insult me,' she thought. Then she spoke, as if from above. 'Whatsoever I have to give, I shall give to those people only. Why should I show it to you?'

Kodai smiled. 'I won't tell anybody about it, my sister-in-law,' he said. 'I am a straightforward man. Now bring that old pot of yours out. For what other occasion would you keep it? No one has given anything yet. How else can we keep the fair name of the village?'

'Do not add insult to injury, my brother-in-law,' said Nohri with a sense of humility. 'Had God left me with something, it wouldn't have been necessary for you even to mention it. At my door saints, ascetics and yogis came, as also the highest officers of State. But not all days are the same.'

Kodai felt ashamed. The wrinkles on his face folded. 'You become grave at something said in jest, sister-in-law,' he said. 'I asked you, lest you should later complain that no one mentioned it to you.'

And having said this, he left. Nohri, however, remained there, following him with her eyes. His sarcasm rankled in her like a poisonous serpent.

While Nohri sat there, a noisy proclamation announced itself. In the west was a cloud of dust, as if the earth were raining dust particles in honour of these pilgrims. Every man and woman in the village left his or her job to go and welcome them. The tricolour was seen fluttering in the breeze, as if Swarajya, seated on a high throne, was showering its blessings on everyone there.

The village women sang songs of welcome. After a while, the group of pilgrims appeared. They marched in rows of twos. Everybody wore khaddar shirts and Gandhi caps. Everyone had bags swinging by their sides, so everyone's hands were free as if ready to embrace Swarajya. Then voices became audible. The masculine throats of the pilgrims sang a fiery song that moved hearts.

'There was a time when we were proud:

But today there is none so disgraced as we;
There was a day when we could sacrifice life for honour;
But today there is none so disgraced as we.'

The village folk advanced several steps to welcome the pilgrims. Their heads were covered in layers of dust, their lips were dry and their faces were tanned, but their eyes glowed with the spark of liberty.

Women sang, children danced with joy, and men fanned visitors with their scarves. No one even thought of Nohri who, with a stick in her hand, stood behind everybody, oozing benevolence. Her eyes were wet and her face shone with pleasure. She looked like a queen to whom the whole village belonged and all the village youngsters were her children. Never before in her life, had she experienced so much energy, pleasure and exhilaration.

Then, all of a sudden, she threw away her stick, cut through the crowd and stood before the pilgrims. It looked as if along with her stick she had also thrown away all her burdens of age and sorrows. She gazed affectionately at the soldiers of freedom infusing as it were, their strength into her. Then she began to dance, and she danced like a pretty young maiden filled with the ecstasy of love and joy. The people retreated a few steps, making a little enclosure for her, and it was in this that the old woman began to display her one-time skill in dancing. In the flood of heavenly ecstasy, she forgot all her grief and misery. No one knew where her enfeebled limbs found so much agility, suppleness and energy from. For some time, people gazed at her in mockery, like children watching the dance of a monkey. But later, the heavenly ecstasy of love inebriated everybody. It seemed to them as if the universe was enveloped within the lap of this embracing dance.

'That's enough, sister-in-law,' said Kodai. 'Let it stop.'

'Why are you standing there?' asked Nohri, slowing down her dance a little. 'Why don't you join me? Let me see how you dance.'

'How can I dance in my old age?' said Kodai.

Nohri paused a little.

'Do you feel old even today?' she asked. 'My old age seems to have given way to youth? Doesn't your chest swell with pride when you see these heroes? It is only to eliminate our misery that they have taken this pledge. All our lives, we have kowtowed to officers and heard their abuses and faced their frowns. At last, all that tyranny will be over soon. Were you and I fit only to become old? Starvation has consumed us all. Can anyone here say that they've had a full meal in the last six months? Has anyone smelt ghee? Has anyone slept peacefully? For fields for which we once paid revenue at the rate of Rs 3, we now pay at nine or ten. Is the earth going to give us gold? We have worked ourselves to exhaustion. We have survived this ordeal; others would have either killed people or got killed themselves. Blessed are the Mahatma and his followers who understand the miseries of the poor and take measures for their removal. Everyone else knows only how to crush us and drain out our blood.'

The faces of the pilgrims brightened up. They chanted with devotion:

'There was a time when in this land flowed rivers of milk and honey.

But today there is none so helpless as us!'

At Kodai's door they burnt torches. People from a number of villages were assembled there. After the pilgrims had partaken of their lunch, the meeting started. The leader of the group stood up and said:

'Brothers, from the welcome and honour you have bestowed upon us, we hope that our chains of slavery will soon be broken. I have seen many countries of the east and west, and I assert from my experience that the simplicity, honesty, hard work and virtues which you have do not exist in any other country in the world. I would even say that you are gods – you are not concerned with luxuries, nor are you addicted to drugs. Devotion to work and contentment with your lot are your ideals. But this godliness and simplicity are proving fatal to your interests. The land revenues are swelling like a river in flood, but you don't protest. The officials and their cronies keep digging their nails into you but you're silent. As a result people are robbing you and you are not even aware of what's happening. Your livelihood is being taken away from you. You are being ruined. But you don't even open your eyes. Formerly, hundreds of thousands of people used to earn a living by spinning and weaving. All the cloth is now being imported from abroad. The manufacture of salt is banned here. Although the salt resources of this country could meet the needs of the world for 200 years, you pay Rs 7,00,00,000 a year for the salt imported into this country. There is salt available in your lakes and fallow lands but you cannot even touch it. After some time, there may be a tax even on your wells. Would you continue to suffer all this injustice?'

'What are we good for?' asked a voice.

The leader replied. 'This is your mistake. It is on your shoulders that this huge empire rests. You are the masters of these great armies and highly placed government servants. And yet, you starve and submit to injustice. Why? Because you are not aware of your own strengths. You must understand that one who cannot defend oneself would always be a victim of the selfish and the unjust. Today, the greatest man of the world is staking his life for you. Thousands of young men are prepared to sacrifice their lives to end your miseries. How would those who think that you are helpless and rob you dry like to see you get out of their clutches? They inflict cruelty on your soldiers. We are prepared to suffer. But you must think of how you can help us. Will you come out like men and save yourself from injustice or will you continue to sit back like cowards and curse your fate? An opportunity like this may never come again. You will always regret it. We are fighting for justice and truth. And we have to fight with weapons of justice and truth. We need heroes who will banish violence and bitterness from their hearts and with complete faith in God, bear anything for what is right. How can you help us?'

No one moved forward. There was pin-drop silence.

Then all of a sudden there was noise. 'The police! The police is here.'

The police inspector, with a posse of constables, came and stood in front of the crowd. The people, with their eyes betraying fright and their hearts beating fast, looked at them and then around us, as if they were looking for a hole to hide themselves in.

'Beat these scoundrels and drive them away,' thundered the inspector.

The constables raised their batons but before they could use them the crowd had dispersed. There was panic. Within ten minutes or so, there was no one from the village.

The leader, however, stood at his post and his group sat behind him. Kodai Chaudhri, of course, sat close to him, staring at the ground intently.

The inspector looked at Kodai sternly.

'Hey, Kodaia,' he asked, 'why have you given shelter to these rogues?'

Kodai turned his reddened eyes towards the inspector, but kept his anger to himself as one ingesting poison. Had he not borne the burden of a family and a business, he would have retorted properly. But his family life, which had consumed fifty years of his life, seem to have coiled round his spirit like a poisonous snake.

Kodai had remained speechless. Nohri appeared from behind. 'Having put on this red turban,' she said, 'your head has turned. Is Kodai your slave that you should address him as Kodaia; you live on our money, and yet you frown on us. Aren't you ashamed of yourself?' Nohri trembled like sunbeams at noon.

For a moment the inspector was stupefied. After some thought, he addressed Kodai.

'Who is this aunt of Satan, Kodai?' he asked. 'If I hadn't had the fear of God, I would have pulled her tongue out from its very root.'

The old woman supported herself with her stick and stared hard at the inspector. 'Why do you disrespect God by uttering His name?' she said. 'Your god is the officer whose boots you lick. You ought to have ended your life in disgrace. Do you know who these people who have come here are? These are the people who are ready to lay down their lives for the sake of us poor. And you call them rogues? – you, who encourage gambling, arrange thefts and dacoities, implicate good men in trouble in order to get money. Yes, you call them rogues?'

Hearing the carping words of Nohri, many who had hidden themselves assembled again. When the inspector saw that the crowd was collecting again, he took out his whip and assaulted them. The people ran helter-skelter again. One lash fell on Nohri. And she felt as though a flame had run down her entire back. There was darkness before her eyes. Nevertheless, she gathered all her strength.

'Why don't you run away, young men?' she screamed. 'Did you come here for a feast? Or was it for some entertainment? It is your own cowardice that has made all these people feel brave like tigers! How long will you tolerate these abuses and kicks?'

One of the constables seized her neck and pushed her hard. When the old woman was about to fall Kodai leapt forward and gave her support.

'Why, friends, should you vent your anger on a poor woman in distress?' Kodai said. 'Has slavery destroyed your manhood? You assault women, old men and the unarmed ones! This does not behove men.'

Nohri lay on the ground. 'Had they been manly,' she said, 'why would they have become slaves? How can man be so cruel? Had an Englishman behaved so cruelly, one could understand, because he is the ruler. But you – you are only his slaves. You will not get any reward. But just as a widow is pleased with little, so are you. You will cut the throats of other people without hesitation, so that you get your wages.'

The inspector now started to reprimand the leader of the group. 'Under whose orders did you enter this village?' he asked.

'The orders of God,' said the leader.

'You are disturbing the peace here,' said the inspector.

'If to make the people conscious of their conditions is to disturb the peace,' said the leader, 'then undoubtedly we are disturbing the peace.'

The panic-stricken crowd again halted. Kodai looked towards them with eyes of despair. 'Brothers,' he said in a trembling voice, 'these are assembled people from many villages. After the insults inflicted on us by the inspector, can you ever sleep peacefully? Who will hear our appeal? Would the officers hear of it? If we were to be killed today, nothing would ever happen! This then is our status and our honour. Shame be on this existence.'

The crowd came to a standstill like flowing water contained by an embankment. The mist of fear, which had overcast the hearts of the people, was suddenly broken. People's faces became stern.

When the inspector noticed their changed attitude, he mounted his horse and ordered that Kodai be arrested. Two constables advanced and caught hold of Kodai's hands.

'Why are you worried?' said Kodai. 'I won't run away. Let us go now. Where do you want to take me?'

As Kodai went with the two constables, his two young sons, as also a number of other people, rushed towards the constables to extricate Kodai from their grip. The people, greatly agitated, closed in around the policemen.

'You had better disperse,' said the inspector. 'Otherwise, I shall fire.'

The crowd retorted by shouting, 'Long live Mother India' and advanced another few steps.

The inspector saw that it would be impossible to get away alive. 'Mr Leader,' he said politely, 'these people are hell-bent on creating trouble and its consequences will not be good.'

'No,' said the leader, 'as long as there is a single one of us here, none will raise his hands against you. We have no enmity with you. We are being trampled under the same feet. It is our misfortune that we stand in opposite camps today.'

As he said this, the leader of the group argued with the villagers. 'Brothers,' he said, 'I have told you that ours is a battle for justice and faith. We have to fight with weapons of justice and faith. We don't have to fight our friends or indeed anyone. If there had been an Englishman in place of this inspector, we would have protected him. The inspector has arrested Kodai Chaudhri, and I consider it the good fortune of the Chaudhri. Blessed are those who are convicted for their work in the battle for freedom. There is nothing to get worried or excited about. Please move on and let the police go.'

The inspector and the police, along with Kodai, left. 'Victory be to Mother India,' shouted the people triumphantly.

'Victory be to Rama, brothers,' said Kodai. 'Victory be to Rama. Stand firm in your struggle. There is nothing to worry about. God is the lord of us all.'

His two sons, with tears in their eyes, approached him. 'What are your instructions for us, father?' they asked in nervous tones.

'Don't lose faith in God,' said Kodai to encourage them. 'Do only what men should do. Fear is the root of all evil. Banish it from your hearts. Nobody will be able to harm you. Truth can never be vanquished.'

The fearlessness which Kodai experienced today, with the policemen around him, was unlike any such experience he ever had before. Prison and the hangman's noose held no fear for him. These, indeed, had become a matter of pride. For the first time in his life, he had seen truth as though it were a protective armour.

To the people of his own village, Kodai's arrest was repulsive. The Chaudhri had been arrested in their very presence and yet they could do nothing. On every face were signs of deep anguish, as though the village had been pillaged.

Then all of a sudden Nohri cried out: 'What are you all regretting now? Have you realized your sad state? Do you still wish for some further proof? We are being ruled not by law, but by force. In spite of this disgrace, we say nothing. Had we not been selfish and cowardly, would they have ever dared flog us? As long as you behave like slaves and continue to serve them, you will get the bare necessities of life. The day you shirk work, however, you'll be beaten up. How long will you live like corpses and be subjected to being eaten up by vultures? Show them that you are alive and that you too have your self-respect. If you are to lose self-respect, why should you do farming or earn money? Why, indeed, should you live? Or do you continue to live so that your children may receive similar kicks and be trampled underfoot. Stop this cowardice. You'll die one day. Why not die like heroes in this battle? I am now an old woman, and if I'm not able to do anything else, I'll sweep the place where these heroes lie down and fan them!'

'If you go with them while we live, aunty,' said Kodai's elder son, Maikoo, 'shame be on us. We, your children, are still alive. I'll go with them and Ganga will look after the farming.'

Ganga, his younger brother, protested. 'This is unjust. So long as I'm alive, you cannot go with them. If you remain here, you can look after the family. That's what I cannot do. Let me go, then.'

'Leave it to aunty to decide,' said Maikoo. 'We shall continue to argue about it. Whoever Nohri orders should go.'

Nohri smiled with pride.

'Whosoever bribes me,' she said, 'shall win.'

'Will there be bribery in your court too, aunty?' asked Maikoo. 'We had hoped that at least in your court there'd be justice.'

'I with a "kingdom" on my deathbed, let me earn something,' said Nohri.

Ganga laughed. 'I shall get you something, aunty,' she said, 'when I go to the market next time. I shall bring you a leaf of tobacco from the eastern provinces.'

'In that case, you win,' said Nohri. 'And it is you who will go.'

'You are not dispensing justice, aunty,' said Maikoo.

'Have the two parties ever welcomed the decision of a court of law?' asked Nohri. 'If none has, how could you?'

Ganga touched Nohri's feet and embraced his brother. 'Please tell father tomorrow,' he said, 'that I am also going.'

'Please enlist my name,' said one. 'My name is Seva Ram.'

All shouted triumphantly, and Seva stood next to the leader.

'Please enlist my name also,' said another one. 'It's Bhajan Singh.'

There was another victorious shout and Bhajan Singh also went and stood close to the leader.

Bhajan Singh was well known in the nearby villages for his wrestling bouts. As he stood close to the leader, with his chest expanded and his head erect, it was as though a new life had arisen in the ceremonial hall.

'Please enlist my name too,' came a third voice. 'It's Ghoore.'

Ghoore was the village watchman. People raised their heads and looked at him in wonder. None could believe that Ghoore too would enlist.

'What has come over you, Ghoore?' asked Bhajan Singh laughing.

'The same,' said Ghoore, 'as has come over you. I have slaved for twenty years, and I am tired of it.'

'Enlist my name also,' came a voice again. 'It's Kale Khan.'

Kale Khan was an attendant of the landlord, aggressive and cruel. The people were surprised at his offer.

'Its seems,' said Maikoo, 'that your house is filled with what you have robbed off us. Isn't that so?'

And Kale Khan replied somewhat gravely: 'Would you never allow a man gone astray to return to the right path? I have obeyed the master whose salt I've eaten, and robbed you to fill his house. Now, however I have realized that I have all along been labouring under a great misconception. I have harassed you a good deal in the past. Please forgive me.'

All the five volunteers embraced each other; they jumped and they shouted, as though they had already won Swarajya. They had won Swarajya, for Swarajya is only an attitude of the mind. As soon as fear born out of slavery is exiled from your heart, you have won Swarajya. Fear is slavery and fearlessness is freedom.

The leader addressed the volunteers. 'Friends,' he said, 'today you have joined the ranks of the soldiers of freedom. I congratulate you. Do you know what sort of battle we are going to wage? You will be subjected to all kinds of hardships. But remember that just as you have today renounced hatred and greed, you will have to give up violence and anger. We are going to fight the battle of Faith, and we have to be firm with regard to our duty. Are you ready for it?'

'We are ready,' all said in unison. Thereupon, the leader blessed them. 'May God help you,' he said.

That glorious golden morning was filled with exultation. Gentle wafts of breeze and the rays of mild light were hallowed. It looked as though the Goddess of Freedom was beckoning them. The farms and fields were unchanged, the gardens and orchards were the same, the men and women were not different, but the blessings, the boons and the richness of this morning had never been felt before. These farms and fields, gardens and orchards, men and women had all been steeped in a new splendour.

Several thousand people had assembled there well before the sun rose. When the soldiers of freedom came out, the sky was rent with the echoes of intoxicated slogans voiced by the people. The farewell scene for the new volunteers, of the determination of their wives, of the moving pride to their parents and of the sacrifice of the fighters exulted the people.

Suddenly Nohri, walking with the help of her stick, came and stood there.

'Aunty,' said Maikoo, 'please give us your blessings.'

'I'll accompany you, my son,' said Nohri. 'And if I do that, how many of my blessings would you ask for?'

'If you go away, Nohri,' said several people in unison, 'who will stay here?'

'It is time for me to go, my sons,' said Nohri, in a tone suffused with good wishes. 'If I don't go today, it'll be another three or four months before I will be able to go. If I go now my life would have been a success. If, however, I pass away in bed after a few months' confinement, my hopes and yearnings will remain with me. All these children are my own. By serving them, I shall obtain deliverance. May God usher in good times for you, and may I be blessed with seeing you happy in my own lifetime.'

And, saying this, Nohri blessed them all, and went and stood close to the leader.

The people watched and the procession moved forward, singing:

> There was a time when we were proud;
> But today there is none so disgraced as we.

Nohri's feet did not touch the earth. It seemed to her as though she was flying in an aeroplane towards heaven.

EIGHTEEN

MADHURI AND NAVAL KISHORE PRESS PROPRIETOR, BISHAN Narain Bhargava, went to Madras for the horse races, but he lost his life there. Following his demise there was a change in the situation in the organization. My link with *Madhuri* was terminated, and the work assigned to me was the preparation of textbooks. In the department of textbooks there was a new development. The manager of the press and leader of a group hostile to me got some support in a new canvasser in the department, Mr Pant. Ever since his appointment, Pant tried to garner control over the management. From day one, when he was posted, he considered me to be his rival and he tried to get me thrown out. A move for economy in the press was already underway. He used the ground to get rid of all the editorial staff and instead of getting books written in the department, he thought he would get the books written by influential people or in the name of members of the textbook committee. Those opposed to me did not appreciate that the salary paid to me could be recovered from the sale of just one book written by me. They hadn't paid me even half of what they had earned from books authored by me and had also overlooked the fact that the royalties to be shelled out to the influential people would have been very steep. If this canvasser had not delayed pushing the books authored by me with the deliberate intention of getting these turned down – the Naval Kishore Press would have earned thousands of rupees. When these books didn't find a place in the list of approved books, he carried on a prolonged correspondence solely with the idea of impressing upon the bosses that he had done his best. I had written out my letter of resignation a year earlier. However, on the advice of friends, I had not forwarded it. I would not have been sorry to leave this place. But owing to human frailties, I felt a little envious of my adversaries prospering at my cost. The depression was killing me.

My Saraswati Press had little work. The journal *Hans* was in the red. The market for novels was very slack. The overall situation was indeed disheartening. Books generally did not sell well. Somehow I managed to just get by. If Maulvi Abdul Haque gave me some translation work or editing or compilation work at reasonable rates, and I got about Rs 500 a year from translations, I might have been comfortable. I now proposed writing some readers (textbooks) which might provide work to the press, and devoted my time in the village to literature. If the readers approved, I would be comfortable for a couple of years. This anyhow was how I felt. What really was to happen was yet to be seen. In any case, I had to leave for Banaras in April…

* * *

Security was demanded from the *Hans*. With the lapse of the ordinance, I had thought that the demand for security would go. Now a new ordinance had been issued and the demand for security renewed. We had started printing the June–July issue. When the manager went to the Magistrate with a fresh declaration for permission to bring out the issue of the journal, the magistrate refused and ordered that security be deposited. I didn't have money or a promissory note and I didn't wish to take a loan. The issue was ready to be dispatched. I sent an application to the government saying:

To
The Collector & Magistrate
Banaras

Sir,

I humbly beg to make the following representation for your favourable consideration:

That I am the proprietor and Editor of a Hindi monthly magazine named Hans, issued from the Saraswati Press, Banaras. It is a social and literary magazine devoted particularly to light literature, occasionally discussing political developments in its columns.

That unfortunately one of its editorial notes published in April 1932, has been objected to by the Government and a security is Rs 1000/- has been demanded from me under the Press ordinance. Not being in a position to furnish the security, I suspended the publication of the magazine in June.

That the said ordinance having expired on 4 July 1932, a declaration was duly filed on the 12 July for the renewal of the magazine, but the permission to republish the magazine has been withheld and the same demand has been renewed in your order dated 2 August 1932.

That with the expiry of the first ordinance the demand of security demanded under the ordinance could not hold good, unless a fresh offence was committed. In that case the renewed ordinance should have been applied.

That the suspension of the magazine for one month and the delay in bringing out the July issue has already caused me serious loss and the purpose of the Government to punish has been thoroughly served. We have also decided to eschew politics from our columns in future.

That the note objected to by the Government was written in a spirit of fair criticism and nothing was farther from my mind than to set at defiance the authority of the Government or to create a hostile impression against it, violence being totally out of question.

That having given an undertaking in our declaration that politics would be totally eschewed in future, there is no justification, I humbly submit, for a renewal of the demand of security. I therefore respectfully request that the security be withdrawn for which I shall feel sincerely grateful.

I have the honor to be Sir,
Your most obedient servant
Sd/-

BANARAS
Dated 9th August 1932.

* * *

Our district officer is a man of learning. He has researched considerably in history and in old coins. How he finds the time for it in the midst of his official duties, I don't know. I have read his works and am a secret admirer of his. His being the district officer is, however, a barrier between us. I am certain that if I took the initiative in meeting him it would, as usual, be misconstrued. I am one of those who do not invite government officials to preside over public functions. Whenever I hear that a school, a hospital or a widow's home has been named after a governor, I feel disgusted.

One day, I was asked by the district officer to come and visit him. I found myself in a predicament. Friends whom I consulted, advised me not to go. Their argument was that if it had been in connection with some official matter then I had no choice. In this case I had been asked to come for a private interview and it was not obligatory for me to go. They even suggested that I had been insulted by being summoned. 'If he is so keen to meet you,' they said, 'why doesn't he come to see you? When will these Indian officers realize that outside the office they are as good or as bad as any other person? They probably cannot forget that they are officers even when they are with their wives.' Another friend who kept a treasure chest of jokes about government officers, related the story of an officer who went to his in-laws to fetch his wife. When the father-in-law insisted that the girl should be allowed to stay on with them for another month, the officer came back furious and issued summons for the arrest of the father-in-law. The next day the old man came with the daughter and begged forgiveness. These district officers were a snooty lot and he advised me to keep away from them. His contention was that since I was not interested in a Naib-Tehsildari or a recommendation for my son, there was precious little that I could expect to gain from his acquaintanceship. If I wrote a story or an article which was considered seditious, I would be arrested and no mercy would be shown to me merely because I knew the district officer.

However, I did not follow the wise counsel of my friends. To turn down a request merely because it was from the district officer, appeared to me to be against good manners. If he had come to see me, it would not have led to loss of prestige for him. A district officer is an important personage in this country and a writer is an ordinary individual. It is not like in England or America where even a Prime Minister would consider it an honour to visit a writer. This is India, where poets crowd around every rich man and writers go uninvited to coronations in the hope of getting a reward. 'He is the district officer,' I said to myself, 'and you are an ordinary writer. When you are so proud of yourself, why shouldn't he be – yes, he who is the virtual king of the district. Whether you call it weakness, foolishness or pride, it is understandable in a man of his position. Besides, if he had come to your house, wouldn't it have created a problem for you? There is not even a decent chair in your house. You are used to twenty-four-for-three-pice bidis. Where would you have got the expensive cigars for him? You do not even know their brand nor where they can be purchased. Thank God he did not come to see you; otherwise you would have had to spend at least four to five rupees, and yet felt that you were not able to entertain him properly. If, because of your bad luck, his wife also came, would your wife have been able to entertain her? One can live in one's own house in rags, but can any self-respecting person bear the thought of making his poverty a topic of drawing-room conversation? You would not have been able to utter a word before his wife and would have prayed for the ground to open up and take you in. With all these considerations in mind, I decided to go and visit the district officer. I stayed with him for some time and we talked about things in general. His attitude did not give me any reason to complain. Although I did not attach any importance to this meeting, it soon came to be known that I was a great friend of the district officer. Some even said that he consulted me on all important matters. A drowning man clutches at a straw. I could have easily taken advantage of the situation. It would not have been difficult for me to convince people that through me, they could get favours from the district officer. Many people came to me – some had grudges against the police, some had tales to tell about the high-handedness of the income-tax officials, others complained about discrimination in the district office where undeserving people were getting promotions. My answer was the same to all of them – that such matters had nothing to do with me.

One day, I was sitting in my room, when a childhood friend visited me. We had studied together. That was some forty-five years earlier. I was then about eight or nine years old. He too was about the same age. I was thin, lean and intelligent. He was fat, strong and dull. Our teacher was completely fed up with him and had assigned me the task of giving him extra lessons. I considered this a great honour and where the teacher's cane failed, my sympathetic approach yielded results. Baldev was soon doing better in studies. Unfortunately, due to the teacher's sudden death, the school closed down and we all parted. Since then I had met Baldev casually only once or twice and had never exchanged more than a mere hurried greeting with him.

Shaking his hand, I said, 'How are you Baldev? Come in. I have not seen you in ages.'

'I have been wanting to see you too, for a long time,' said Baldev. 'You are my teacher, you know. But for you, I would still be a good-for-nothing chap. Now I can at least look after my lands. I don't know why, but whatever the Maulvi Sahib taught me went completely over my head. For teaching an ass like me, the credit goes entirely to you.'

'Baldev,' I said, overwhelmed, 'whenever I see you, childhood memories come back afresh and this long period of forty-five years vanishes in a minute.'

Baldev replied, 'You know, I have always regarded you as an elder brother, and I tell everyone that I can depend on you whenever I am in trouble. You are thin as ever. Why don't you eat proper food? If you can't get good ghee I can send you a couple of tins. Remember you are getting old and food is the only thing that will keep you going. Look at me. I can still drink a seer of milk and eat a quarter seer of ghee besides some butter. I have to keep fit. My whole life has been devoted to bringing up the children, but do they care about me? If I were to fall ill they would not even come to ask if I needed anything. Yes, I had come to you about my eldest son. He is also a hefty and well-built man like me, and can never take anything lying down. On a number of occasions he quarrelled with the police and they have always been on the lookout for an opportunity to implicate him. Recently when a dacoity took place in the village, they got their chance and during the investigations roped him in. He is under arrest and has been in jail since last week. The case is filed in the court of the Deputy Collector, Mr Mohammed Khalil. The Daroga Sahib and he are great friends and I am sure that my son will be sentenced. No one but you can save him. If he is sentenced, the whole family will be ruined. I do not expect you to go out of your way. All I want is for the district officer to know that it is a completely false case and that he should investigate the matter personally. I know that you are a childhood friend of mine and my guru. Please don't refuse. You do not like getting involved in such matters. But in this case, consider that your own son is in trouble. If the case had not been absolutely false, I would not have troubled you. The boy's mother is crying her heart out. His wife has not eaten anything since his arrest. Nothing has been cooked in the house since he was taken away. If he is sentenced, I am sure that both these women will die. I have consoled them by saying that as long as you are alive, no one can harm the boy.'

I was in a dilemma. All the objections that I could have put forward had already been answered by Baldev Singh. I could not think of a valid excuse to get out of the predicament.

I eventually said, 'All right, I shall mention it to the district officer, but it is doubtful that anything will come out of it. He does not interfere in the work of his subordinates.'

'You go and tell him about this case,' repeated Baldev Singh, 'that is all that I am asking of you to do. The rest will depend on fate. Will you go tomorrow?'

'Yes,' I replied, 'I will go and see him tomorrow.'

I was busy writing and then, after finishing my meal, lay down to rest. I had no intention of keeping my promise to him. All I had to tell him when I met him next was that the district officer did not consider it proper to interfere in the case....

I had completely forgotten about the incident when, eight days later, Baldev Singh and his son came to see me. The son knelt and touched my feet. Baldev Singh said, 'This is the boy. He has been let off without a blemish. The district officer called the Daroga Sahib and reprimanded him severely, warning him that if in future he indulged in maligning innocent and respectable people, he would be dismissed. The Daroga could not even show his face to me after this. It is all due to you. But for you, we would have been undone. You have saved four lives. When I came to you, I had my doubts whether you will help. People had told me that nobody had ever benefitted through you, but I was certain that you would not let me down.'

And, saying this, he signalled to his son, who went out and brought a huge bundle of presents. In spite of my refusal they refused to take them back. I could not gather the courage to tell them that I had done nothing to deserve this reward.

NINETEEN

BACK IN BANARAS, THE SARASWATI PRESS DID NOT HAVE MUCH work. I, therefore, started the *Hans*. This decision was also foolish. The *Hans* too became a headache, and there was little profit. It incurred losses of Rs 4000–5000. Then I got the idea of a weekly into my head.

I had suffered losses of several thousand rupees, but I could not resist the temptation of having a weekly of my own. I therefore took over *Jagaran*. This cost me several thousands. My whole life has been full of losses. If these journals had run there would not have been difficulties of work for the press.

Neither of the journals has been a success. All that I earned from my books was spent to meet the liabilities of these journals. The weekly was proving a headache. Its print order was 2000 and all the copies got sold out, but there was little advertisement and it was losing Rs 1500. The burden of the weekly *Jagaran* became unbearable. I had to extricate myself from the situation. It was a mistake to have started it. My ego in the way of my closing it down. People would make fun of me... I wish I had the courage to close it down, but I could not muster it.

Financially, I have been a failure. I did not understand business and penury has never forsaken me. I was never a journalist, but circumstances forced me to become one. And I lost all that I earned from literature – not much the first place – on these two journals.

I got Rs 500 for *Sevasadan*. It was translated into Gujarati and I got Rs 100. Film rights of *Sevasadan* got me Rs 750. Hindi Pustak Agency gave me a lump sum of Rs 3000 for *Prem Pachisi, Sapta Saroj, Premashram* and *Sangram*. For *Nav Nidhi* I got Rs 200. Dulareylal Bhargava gave me Rs 1800 for *Rangabhoomi*. For anthologies of short stories I got Rs 200. I myself published *Kayakalp, Azad Katha, Prem Thirtha, Prem Pratima* and *Pratigya*. It would have added up to not more than Rs 6000.

Editions of my works in other languages have been mostly in Urdu, followed by Marathi and Gujarati. The Urdu translation of *Rangabhoomi* got me Rs 800. No other publisher was willing to undertake its publication but a Gujarati publisher agreed to give me Rs 400 for *Rangabhoomi*. People approached me for the rights of *Premsharan* in Telugu and Tamil.

An Urdu publisher of Lahore owed me thousands. After several reminders over the years, I realized that this amount would not be realized. A legal notice might bring me something.

I wrote to Lajpat Rai and Sons in Lahore to pay me in instalments. No reply. The sum involved was Rs 800. There are publishers in Lahore who have not paid huge amounts. I will be forced to send a registered letter.

Three or four of my stories have been translated into Japanese. For these Sabbarwal sent me Rs 50. Miscellaneous income would not be more than Rs 25 per month. As for translations, I will not get more than Rs 2000.

I translated *Silver Box* and *Justice* into Hindi. It was an exacting assignment. I had to ensure that the use of Sanskrit words was avoided, so also of unfamiliar Persian words. For every sentence, I had to spend hours on end. In one sitting, I could perhaps do four or five pages of *Justice*, and I did not get time for more than one sitting a day because if I translated in the mornings, my *Karmabhoomi* would suffer.

As far as financial success is concerned, this commodity is rare in Hindi or Urdu. You may get famous, but by no means could you be financially independent. Our people do not have a weakness for books. It is a result of apathy, dull-headedness and intellectual lethargy.

We have not yet made literature a vocation. Poor Rudra Narayan Aggarwal has contracted tuberculosis and is in the TB hospital at Lucknow. There is no one to help him, none even to sympathize with him. And there would be very few people who are as hard working as him. He translated *War and Peace, Resurrection, Vanity Fair*, etc. Except for *Resurrection,* none of the others have been published so far. They all lie with the publishers. And the poor translator is on his deathbed. Such is the state of literature.

No writer of Hindi has so far made a special study of any segment of society. Ugra did it, but he went astray. I took up only the peasantry. There are many segments of society on which attention needs to be focussed. No writer so far has touched the segment of sadhus. In most of us, there is a predominance of imagination but not enough involvement. I gave away the rights of my early works.

If the publishers are charitably disposed and publish the stories on charitable grounds, then I too shall not expect anything, but if they bring out the edition from a commercial point of view then I as an author can by no means give up my portion of the profits, which must be settled beforehand.

My *Zanzir-I-Havas* is not really a historical story nor is it related to any historical event. However, the name of its hero Qasim is the name of the conqueror of Sindh and there was also an incident in his life which could be used in a short story. But this story of mine has nothing to do with all that. I have not referred to the king of Delhi, to ensure that there is no misunderstanding. Nor have I referred to the then ruler of Multan. The object of my story was only to depict how one gets deeply obsessed with passion and how that obsession becomes intense. I am very fond of my story *Manzil-I-Maqsood.* Many of my Muslim friends praised it and I often wished to write more in that strain. But my pen did not move. It hasn't been translated into Hindi as yet because in its translation, the beauty of it would have been lost. *Daftary* is taken from life. This also suffered a loss of Rs 3000. I had hoped it would give me some regular income. I have made many foolish mistakes. This was another one. I have never had any success so far. Nor do I see any prospects of success. I was never a businessman.

The total number of my short stories reaches an approximate figure of 250. Among my popular short stories are *Bade Ghar Ki Beti, Rani Sarandha, Namak Ka Daroga, Saut, Abhishaap, Prayashchit, Kamanataru, Satyagraha, Mandir aur Masjid, Ghaswali, Mahatirtha, Laanchhan, Sati, Laila*, etc.

TWENTY

I ALWAYS WEAVE PLOTS WITH A VIEW TO BRING OUT WHAT IS beautiful and manly in human character. It is a complicated process, sometimes inspired by a person, an incident or a dream. My stories are generally based on some observation or experience, and I try to inject an element of the drama in them. I never write a story only to portray an event. Instead, I attempt to inject some philosophical or emotional truth into my stories. So long as I do not find some such element for the basis of my story, my pen does not move. Once the spadework has been done, I create the characters of the proposed short story fast. A study of history at times also suggests plots.

I wrote a short story in Hindi. It was captioned the *Queen of Hearts*. In a book of history, I had read of an incident in Timur's life in which there was a mention of his marriage to Hamida Begum. I thought of the dramatic angle of this event. How to create the climax in a historical event was the question. In her earlier years, Hamida Begum had been trained by her father in the art of war. And she had some actual experience of the battlefield also. Timur had massacred thousands of Turks. How could a Turk woman fall for such an enemy of the Turkish people? If this puzzle could be solved, the climax was possible. Now Timur was not good-looking. It was necessary to introduce moral and emotional qualities in him, which could win over an idealistic woman. That's how the story got intricately woven.

Here is the story:

> The brave Turks, before whose might the Christian world trembled at one time, had their blood flowing in the streets of Constantinople. Constantinople had been a victim of Turkish tyranny 100 years earlier and now had the solace of tasting their blood. Several thousand corpses of Turkish soldiers were floating on the waves of the Straits of Bosphorus, and the Turkish army chief, with 100,000 soldiers, was standing before the great Timur for a decision on his future.

'What do you want, life or death,' thundered the victorious Timur, eyeing Yazdani with contempt.

Yazdani raised his head proudly and said, 'If I can lead a life with honour then I want life, otherwise death.'

Timur's anger rose. He had humbled the pride of many kings. He was not used to hearing such words. He had the lives of 100,000 Turks in his hands. He could trample them in one moment. And yet he saw Yazdani asserting himself and asking for a life with honour which meant a life of indulgence, living at the cost of the poor, a life of fun with the beauties from Armenia and Caucasus. No, Timur had not humbled Khalifa Bayazid so that the Turks in the name of Islam and freedom disgraced Islam. Why should so much blood be shed? The flow of human blood is a horrible sight from which eyes turn away and heads bow down in shame. Timur was not an animal who would sacrifice his life to see such a horrible scene. He spoke deprecatingly and said, 'What you call a life with honour is a life of sin and evil.'

Yazdani had not hoped for pity or compassion from Timur. His life and the life of his ranks, he knew, would not be spared. Why should he yield and dare to express freely the hatred in his heart. He looked back sheepishly at the handsome young man who stood behind him, holding back the reins of his youth. His body emitted sparks of anger like steel being powdered by a grindstone. Yazdani saw him and, drawing his sword from the scabbard, he spoke in desperation; 'Sire, you are now a victor, but if you pardon my speaking freely, the Turks do not require to be preached to by the Tartars. In the fallow plains of Tartary, cutoff from the rest of the world, one is prone to lead a life of renunciation or piety, or to eschew the good things of life. But in a place blessed by the Almighty, with all the good things of life, to renounce them would be a sign of ingratitude. If the wielding of a sword be the mark of civilization, then the Gauls would have been much more civilized than the Romans.'

Timur laughed loudly and his soldiers put their hands on their swords, because Timur's laughter meant the laughter of death.

'Are the Tartars mere animals?' he asked.

'No, that is not what I meant,' said Yazdani.

'You said that God has brought you into this world in order to enjoy the pleasures of this world,' said Timur. 'That, I say, is kufra. God has created man to serve mankind and anyone who acts contrarily is indulging in kufra. He deserves to go to hell. The Prophet had come into the world to purify our lives, to make us true men, not to preach sinfulness. Timur has now vowed to rid this world of kufra…'

'The great Prophet, I am not cruel, ferocious and without pity. But, according to me, the punishment for kufra is nothing short of death.'

And he looked towards the Tartar soldiers with murderous looks, and immediately then a giant of a man, wielding his sword, advanced towards Yazdani. The forces of Tartary took out their swords and swooped on the Turks and in no time there were corpses of Turks strewn in the battlefield.

***

Suddenly then, the handsome youth who had been standing behind Yazdani, advanced to Timur and, as if holding life in his clenched fist, said, 'I ask you, oh King, you who calls yourself a Muslim, is this the Islam which you have taken a vow to propagate? Does Islam preach for you to shed the blood of those whose only crime is that they stand for the Khalifa and their country?'

There was pin-drop silence all around. Here was a man, still in his teens, who dared to speak before the mighty Timur without his tongue being pulled out. Those present were all stunned, and Timur stood mesmerized looking at this youth.

The youth looked at the Tartar soldiers, who were all baffled, and said, 'You call these (Turkish) Muslims kafirs and think that by killing them you will be serving God and Islam. If those who have never bowed before anyone other than God, who consider the Holy Prophet as their guide, are not Muslims then who are Muslims? We may be kafirs, I tell you, but we are your prisoners now. Does Islam allow you to kill prisoners in chains? If God has given you the powers, has He given you the right to put to death His own creations? Will you, by killing the sinful, take them onto the path of righteousness? You have got 70,000 brave Turks killed by treachery, blown to death by mines. Can you estimate the number of innocent children rendered orphans, innocent women rendered helpless? Are these then your achievements on the basis of which you proudly call yourself Muslims? And do you leave for posterity your name written in the ink of blood, cruelty and death? Not only have your horses waded through the rivers of blood of the Turks, but you have uprooted Islam too. It was the sacrifice of brave Turk soldiers that conveyed the message of Islam to Europe. And it is because of them that today in the churches of Sophia you hear the call of "Allah O Akbar", and that the whole of Europe is ready to embrace Islam. Do these achievements deserve only death as their reward? You are not preaching the message of Islam by shedding blood. Remember that one day, you will have to give an account of your action before the Almighty. No excuses will be entertained there. If one could differentiate between the good and evil, one should ask oneself, 'Did you undertake this crusade for the sake of good or for the satisfaction of your ego?' The reply you would get will make you bow your heads in shame.'

Timur's head was bent low when Yazdani, trembling, said, 'Lord of the World, I am the father of your servant. He is still in his teens. Please forgive him for his brashness. I am prepared to suffer the consequences.'

Timur fixed his gaze on the face of the youth. It was the first time in his life that he had been spoken to in such a fearless manner. Commanders, ministers and kings dared not protest in his presence. Whatever he said or did was law. He genuinely believed that God had sent him into the world, to awaken Islam and to reform it. Timur had never claimed prophethood but his belief in himself was firm. When this youth staked his life and pierced the veil of Timur's fame, the latter's consciousness dawned. A feeling of respect instead of anger and violence surged. Just one stare from him could mean the end of this youth's life. It looked as if this youth was standing there to control the world conqueror's might. Timur, facing the youth, felt small. The source of such courage in anyone can be based only on faith and the base of that faith is only truth. He was a simple-hearted soldier who, through faith, could convert falsehood into truth.

Yazdani said: 'Lord of the World, please don't mind his bluntness.'

Timur got up from his throne, advanced and embraced Yazdani and the youth. 'I wish I had had occasion earlier, to hear such blunt and insolent words,' said Timur. 'If that had happened, I would not bear the burden of the death of innocents. I see in this youth, the soul of an angel, sent to show the true path to misguided people. You, my friend, are lucky to be the father of such an angel-like son. May I ask you his name?'

Yazdani was an idol worshipper. Then he became a Muslim. Doubts about whether he had done the right thing to embrace Islam did arise in his mind. To a prisoner condemned to death and standing on the scaffold awaiting the unloosening of the rope, it seemed that an angel had come to carry him away. Touched deeply, he said: 'We call him Habib' (Dear one).

Timur advanced towards the youth, caught hold of his hand and raised it to his eyes and said, 'My young friend, you are the dear one of God. I am that sinner who because of his ignorance considered sins to be virtues, because I was told that I could do no wrong. Today I have realized what harm I have brought to Islam. I seek refuge in you. From this day, you are my master, you are my guide. I am now convinced that it is only through you that I can reach the abode of God.' And, saying this, he gazed at the face of the youth who looked shy and modest. Instead of harshness, there was hesitation.

Timur pulled him and made him sit next to himself on the throne. He then ordered the commander of his forces to release all the Turk prisoners, to have their arms restored and to share whatever had been looted equitably by the soldiers.

While his deputy got busy carrying out Timur's orders, Timur took Habib's hands and led him to his tent and ordered that arrangements be made for the hospitality of the two guests. After dinner, he narrated the story of his own life. He wept when he narrated his tale of barbarity. He finally said to Habib: 'My young friend, you will lead me now. You have shown me the path to reach my destination. You can now take over my kingship. I know that I was being led in the direction of destruction. My request to you is that you take over the reins of governance. Please don't say no, for then I'll be nowhere.'

Yazdani submitted, 'It is very graceful of you to bestow on him such favours. But the boy is still young. How will he discharge the duties of governance? This is his age for education.'

While Yazdani insisted on his refusal, Timur continued to insist on compliance with his request. Although Yazdani refused, he was very happy. Moses had gone to get fire, but got prophethood. What he entered the jaws of death, he became a king. Yazdani had confidence in Habib's ability to handle the situation, but he was afraid that in a foreign city he may falter. There are always conspiracies at regal courts. Habib was noble-hearted and intelligent, but where would he have the experience that comes with age? He asked for a day's time to decide and took leave.

***

Habib was Yazdani's daughter, not his son. Her full name was Ummatul Habib. When Yazdani and his wife embraced Islam, their daughter was about twelve years of age. Nature had endowed her with intelligence and a rare intellect, but also with independent ideas. She would not accept anything without thinking about it. Her parent's conversion of faith had caused her some doubts and until she studied Islam deeply she would not, just to please her parents, be initiated into Islam. The parents also did not put pressure on her. They agreed that as they had the right to get converted, she too had her right to adopt any faith. She undertook a comparative study of the scriptures of Islam as well of Zarathustra. After two years of deep study, research and experimentation of the two faiths, she embraced Islam. The parents were indeed happy. Yazdani did not have a son. It was a time when every man relied upon having a son without whom he considered himself unfortunate. Yazdani made up for not having had a son by his daughter. She was imparted an education in the same way as a son would have been. She wore boy's clothes, rode horses and learnt how to use arms. She visited Khalifa Bayazid's palace along with her father and accompanied the Khalifa's sons, princes, for shikaar. She also studied philosophy, poetry and science. In her sixteenth year, she entered the military academy and within two years, passed the highest examination and joined the army. In martial arts and army strategy, she had such competence, that even the Khalifa Bayazid was happy with her progress and gave her the command of 1,000 soldiers. There was no paucity of suitable young men to marry her. Many officer colleagues and youth of royal lineage were prepared to lay down their lives to get her hand, but she showed no interest in any of them. Many proposals for marriage were received every day, but she turned them all down. She was not inclined to get married. Her independent outlook kept her from succumbing to any temptation. She was aware that young girls were brought into families with great pomp and show but then within the palaces, their fate was at the mercies of their husbands. They were denied even the opportunity of socializing with the women of high families. After hearing from them pitiable tales of their experiences, she didn't want dependence after marriage. And Yazdani had no intention of putting curbs on her freedom.

'The girl is independent,' he would say, 'and it is entirely up to her to get married or stay unmarried. She is free to decide for herself.'

Whenever he got proposals, he would tell the suitors, 'I can't decide anything. The decision is entirely hers.'

Even though it was against the tradition for a woman should dress as a man and meet and socialize with men, Yazdani and his wife had no doubts about their daughter's character. In her dealings or behaviour, there was never the least apprehension. This twenty-four-year-old virgin faced the storm of adolescence and temptations unyieldingly, treating all the young men around her as her brothers.

***

The wave of happiness and joy that swept Constantinople, the welcome and flowers showered on Habib and the congratulations heaped on her were beyond description. If she had not done what she did, it is possible that the palaces and the bazaars would have been engulfed in fire. The person who saved the state and the city from that innocent disaster was given honours and affection. The women of the metropolis blessed her from their hearts, and considered themselves lucky to have had a glimpse of her. She had enabled them to raise their heads with pride.

In the night, there were serious deliberations over Timur's proposal.

On the thickly cushioned diwan sat Yazdani, impressive, mighty and composed. On his right, sat his wife dressed in Iranian garments, her eyes full of confidence and compassion. And on his left, sat Ummatul Habib, dressed like a charming bride.

Opposing the offer of Timur, Yazdani said, 'If I am given the right to offer advice, then I would suggest that you don't accept this proposal. The fact is that what you really are, cannot be kept a secret from Timur for any length of time. I don't know what the position would be when it is out. So long as I am here, none dare malign you. But there you would be all alone and slanderers will have their full play.'

Yazdani's wife did not attach any importance to the right to decide for oneself. 'Timur is not at all a good man,' she said. 'I will not allow you to go with him. Something may happen that may make you the world's laughing stock. And aren't there already many who talk slander?'

Habib sat quietly all the while. Yazdani thought that Habib was in agreement with his views. He was ready to convey his rejection of Timur's offer when Habib asked, 'What would you say to Timur?'

'All that has now been decided here.'

'But I haven't said anything.'

'I thought you had agreed with us.'

'No. Please go to him and tell him that I accept the offer.'

Her mother put her hands on her breast and said, 'What are you saying, my daughter. This is terrible. Just think of what the people would say.'

Yazdani held his head in his hands, as if a bullet had pierced his heart. He could not utter a word.

Habib knitted her eyebrows and said, 'Dear mother, I don't at all deviate from whatever be your command. You have every right to decide whether you allow me to go. But in this life, I will never get such a chance to serve the country. For the rest of my life I will repent letting this opportunity go. I have full confidence that with my integrity, devotion and selflessness, I can make Timur a good human being, and perhaps he would never shed so much blood again. He is brave but not heartless. No brave man can truly be heartless. Whatever he has done so far has been as a result of blind faith in religion. Now God has given me an opportunity to show to him that religion means service for the people, not loot and bloodshed. I have not the least doubt in my capability. I can defend myself. And I can claim that by doing my duty honestly, I will be able to make the people shut their mouths up. The principles which I have followed haven't ever let me down. And it is only because of that I have achieved success. My achievements have not even been dreamt of by most people. These can never let me down. If my real identity is known by Timur, why should you worry? My sword can protect my honour. You are aware of my views with regard to wedlock. If I ever meet a man who my inner self accepts and with whom my soul, by sacrificing my own identity, can rise higher, I will fall at his feet and sacrifice my life.'

Yazdani was pleased to hear all this and hugged his daughter, but his wife was not as easily placated. She didn't want to leave her daughter by herself. She would accompany her.

***

Several months later, the youthful Habib was Timur's wazir; but in reality she was the all-in-all, the king. She was the eyes of Timur, she was the ears of Timur. Timur thought with Habib and was guided by Habib. He wanted Habib to be with him all the time. In her company, he felt he was in heaven. There was not a single inhabitant of Samarkand who was jealous of Habib; her dealings won over all of them because the wazir never deviated from justice. Those who got ground down in Habib's mill of justice also had goodwill for her because she did not allow justice to be unnecessarily bitter.

It was dusk time. The officers had left. Lamps had been lit. The scent of agarbatti pervaded the darbar. Habib was getting ready to leave when the chamberlain announced that the Lord of the World was coming. This news did not please Habib much.

Unlike the other minister she wasn't keen for Timur's company. She tried to keep some distance from him. There was never an occasion when he dined at the royal dining table. She seldom participated in the sittings at Timur's palace. When Habib was at peace with herself she narrated the day's activities to the mother.

Habib advanced and welcomed Timur. Timur took his seat on the throne and addressed Habib, 'I am surprised that you, still a youth, are living the life of an ascetic. The Almighty has given you such marvellous looks that the prettiest woman would consider herself lucky to be your beloved. I don't know whether you are aware, that when you ride your beautiful horse, thousands of eyes peep through windows, keen to have a glimpse of you. But no one has seen you look up. The more I try to follow your footsteps, the less I am allowed to do so. Why don't you allow the magic of your purity to influence me? I wish to live like you, to be a part of this world and yet out of it. But I have neither the heart nor the intellect.

'I am thirsty for human blood which you don't allow to be quenched. And knowing that whatever you do, none can do better, I cannot control my anger. Whichever way you pass, you shed love and light. Even one who should be your enemy, becomes your friend. Where I go, I spread hatred and fear. And one who should be my friend, becomes my enemy. This is the only place in the world, where I have some peace. If you think that the crown and the throne are obstacles in the way of my salvation, then I can kick them today. I have come to you today to ask that you show me the way to real happiness. I wish you to stay in this palace, so that I can learn from you what true life is.'

Habib's heart beat fast. 'Does it mean that the Amir has come to know of my identity as a woman?' Habib did not know how to reply. Seeing Timur's self-pity, her sensitive heart melted. The man at the mention of whose name the world trembled, was standing before her, begging for mercy, benediction. In the cruel, perverted, violence-ridden personality of Timur, Habib saw a ray of hope. He thought poorly of his own stale life, there was no room for ascending higher.

Greatly touched, Habib said, 'Sir, that you think so highly of me is my great fortune. But it is not appropriate for me to stay in the royal palace.'

'Why not?' asked Timur.

'Where there is great wealth, there are dacoities too, and in a palace where there is honour, enemies abound.'

'Can there be an enemy of yours?'

'I shall be my own enemy. The greatest enemy of man is his pride.'

Timur looked as if he had got a great gem. He became aware of himself. He pondered over the remark that the greatest enemy of man is his pride. He repeated it to himself several times and then said, 'I'll never get you Habib, never. You are a bird that can fly only in the sky. If you put it in a cage of gold it would flutter. Thanks be to you, my guide.'

Timur left for his palace, as if to put the philosophy in safe custody. It wasn't the first time that he had heard this sentence but this time it conveyed to him a message of wisdom, command and goodwill, which he had never experienced before.

***

A report was received of a revolt in the Esthaka area of the kingdom. Habib mused that Timur might go there and order mass killings. She was keen to solve the problem through peaceful means and thus show to Timur how powerful the force of goodwill was.

Timur was reluctant to send Habib on this expedition, but in the face of Habib's insistence, he was helpless. When Habib could not think of any other reason she said to Timur, 'So long as your slave (myself) is there, why should you endanger your life? No, you cannot go there.'

Timur smiled. 'There is little value of my life as against yours, Habib,' he said. 'And I have never cared for my own life. What I am leaving behind are only memories of bloodshed, loot and arson. With my demise no one would shed tears for me. Looters like me would continue to be born. If our enemies succeed, then this empire will disintegrate and the only thing for me would be to thrust a knife into my own body. I cannot tell you, Habib, how much I have gained from you. If I had met you five or ten years earlier, then Timur's name would not have been blackened in history. Today, if need be, I could sacrifice a thousand Timurs at your feet. You are taking my soul with you. I tell you today, Habib, that I love you. I've never had such love for the prettiest woman. What love is I do not know. But where is the harm if I come along with you?'

'If I think I need you,' said Habib, 'I will let you know.'

'As you wish,' said Timur, putting his hand on his beard. 'But do send me a daily report through a messenger, lest I get panicky and come down there.'

Timur made all the arrangements for Habib's departure. He collected many articles of daily use for her comfort. For where, in the desert, would she get all these. He was as involved, as a mother sending her daughter away to her in-laws would be.

When Habib left in command of the army, the whole of Samarkand came out to see her off. Timur sat on his throne, covering his eyes with a handkerchief, his head bent like an injured bird.

***

Esthakhar was an area inhabited by Armenian Christians. Muslims had conquered this area and they had promulgated measures which made the Christians remember at almost every step, that they were a defeated people. The first measure was the imposition of Jaziya which all non-Muslims were obliged to pay. The other measure was that no bells were to be rung in the churches. The Christians opposed these measures and the Muslim rulers used force to carry them out. The Christians then revolted. The Muslim subedar was arrested and on the fort flew the Christian flag.

This was Habib's second day here. The issue had to be resolved.

Her large-heartedness told her that the restrictions on the Christians were uncalled for. Every faith should enjoy the same respect. The Muslims would never agree to lift these restrictions. Even if the Muslims agreed, why should Timur agree? There were always some differences of views with regard to religious matters. Timur may not agree to lift these restrictions. Should Habib punish the Christians only because they were fighting for independence? And should she sacrifice what she thinks is truth? She would follow the true path whatever the consequences. 'The Amir might think that I was crossing the limits, but that does not matter,' she thought. The following day, therefore, Habib had an announcement made by the beat of the drum that Jaziya be removed, and there would be no restrictions on drinking nor ringing bells in churches.

There was commotion among the Muslims. This, they said, was kufra. Idol worshipping was sin. Islam, which Amir Timur had established by shedding blood, was being uprooted by his wazir, Habib Pasha. The situation then took a turn. The royal forces now joined the Muslims.

Habib took refuge in the fort of Esthakhar. There was an increase in the strength of the Muslim forces. They surrounded the fort. Thinking that Habib had revolted against Timur, they sent a messenger to Timur to convey to him the news and to let him know the situation as it was.

***

It was past midnight. Timur had no news from Esthakhar for two days. He had all sorts of apprehensions. And he was regretting that he had allowed Habib to go alone, even though he knew that Habib was very clever. If the rebels are in great strength, he thought, what could Habib with a small force do? The revolt could certainly get serious. The Christians of Esthakhar were a very determined lot... When they felt that Timur's sword was rusted and that he now prefered life in palaces, they would become emboldened. And if Habib was surrounded by enemies it would be terrible.

He showed his irritation. Why had he become so defeat prone? Had his glory and bravery left him? He, the mention of whose name would make enemies tremble, was today hiding in palaces? The only message to the world was that Timur is not the hero of the battlefield, but of carpets in the palaces. Habib was an angel; he did not know the wiles of men. The angel, with pity, compassion and selflessness, did not know that man can behave like Satan. In peace time, these qualities take a nation onto the path of progress. In a war, when waves of satanic proportions take over, there is no place for such qualities. Then you talk only of those who shed human blood, put fields and forests on fire and convert habitations into wilderness. The rules of peace are different from the rules of war.

Suddenly then, the chamberlain announced the arrival of a messenger from Esthakhar. Ushered in, the messenger kissed the earth, and stood on one side. Such was his awe of Timur, that he forgot what he had come to communicate. Knitting his eyebrows,

Timur asked him the message he had brought. 'You have come after three days, which is two days too late and that too at night.' The messenger kissed the earth again and said, 'The representative of God on earth, sire, the wazir, has waived the imposition of Jaziya.'

'What do you say?' thundered Timur 'He has withdrawn Jaziya?'

'Yes, Sire.'

'Who has done it?'

'The wazir, Sire.'

'On whose orders?'

'His own authority.'

'I see.'

'And sire, he has allowed the use of alcohol too.'

'I see.'

'He has permitted the ringing of bells in the churches.'

'I see.'

'And sire, he has joined hands with the Christians against the Muslims.'

'What can I do then?'

'You are our lord, Sire. If we do not get reinforcements, not a single Muslim would be left alive.'

'Where is Habib Pasha at this time?'

'In the fort of Esthakhar.'

'And what are the Muslim forces doing?'

'They have surrounded the Christians in the fort.'

'Along with Habib?'

'Yes, Sire, he has joined the rebels against you.'

My faithful Muslim soldiers have made him a prisoner?

'It is possible, Sire, that before I return, they would have put him to death.'

'Get out of my sight, you wretched fellow,' said Timur. 'The Muslims think that Habib is my employee, and I am his master.

This is wrong. This is a lie. Habib is the lord of the kingdom. Timur is a humble follower of his. Timur cannot disagree with his decisions. Jaziya, I say, must go. I have really no right to ask Christians to pay the price for following their own faith. If azaan is allowed in the mosques, there is no reason why the church bells should not be rung. The call of the church bells is not kufra. Do you hear me, you wretched fellow. There is no kufra in the church bells. The kafir is one who robs others of their rights, tyrannizes the poor, deceives others or is selfish. A kafir is not one who sees the image of God in a clay or stone idol, or who sees the glory of God in rivers and mountains, in trees and bushes. He is a greater devotee of God than people like us, who think of God imprisoned in the precincts of the mosque. You seem to think what I am saying is kufra? To consider anyone as kafir is kufra. We all are the creations of God, devotees of God. That's all. Go now and tell the rebel Muslims that if they don't raise the siege, Timur will reach there, and it would be their doomsday.'

The messenger stood stunned. He suddenly heard the army bugles sounding outside and the forces getting ready for the expedition. After three days, Timur reached Esthakhar. The siege of the fort had been lifted. The guns in the fort welcomed his arrival. While Habib thought that Timur had arrived to punish the Christians, the Christians were in panic.

Habib too was ready for a confrontation. To save the Christians, she was ready to lay down her life. There can be no compromise on this issue, he said to himself. If Timur took recourse to the use of sword, what was happening there? I see the royal force holding the white flag! Timur has come, not to fight, but to compromise. His welcome would then be of a different type. Habib, accompanied by Christian leaders, came out of the fort. Timur advanced on his horse alone. Habib dismounted from his horse and paid obeisance to Timur who also dismounted from the horse, kissed Habib on his forehead and said, 'I have heard everything, Habib. You have done the right thing. You have done what only you could have done. I had really no right to impose Jaziya or to deny Christians their religious rights. I will hold a darbar today and announce my approval of these measures. I will also propose something that I have been wanting to do for quite some time and I hope that you will accept it. No, you will have to accept it.'

Habib was taken aback. 'Has the truth become known to him?' she asked herself. What is his proposal? Habib's heart pounded fast.

Timur smiled and asked Habib, 'Tell me, were you prepared to fight against me?'

'Truth is supreme,' said Habib with all modesty, 'even more than Timur's personality.'

'Certainly, certainly,' said Timur, 'for you have the heart of angels, and also the courage of a lion. My only regret is that you presumed that Timur would reverse your decisions. For, it is you who has made me realize that this kingdom is not my ancestral property but is like a tree, each branch, each leaf of which is entitled to draw sustenance.'

The two entered the fort together. The sun had set. Within moments a darbar was held and Timur announced that he agreed to the rights of the Christians. 'Long live the emperor,' shouted everybody.

Then Timur said, 'Friends, I am not entitled to the blessings that you have given me. While I return what I had forcibly taken away from you, I do not think I deserve your prayers or blessings. What would really be appropriate is that you reproach me for denying you your rights for so long.'

'Cries of "Marhaba, Marhaba" rent the air.

'I return to you, not only your rights, but also your country because, in the eyes of God, all human beings are the same. And no nation or individual is really entitled to rule over others. You are your own rulers and I hope that you will not deny the Muslims their rights. If ever there is occasion when some aggressor tries to rob you of your freedom, Timur will be ready to come to your aid.'

The celebrations in the fort were over. The officers and all those present took leave. Only Timur and Habib were left by themselves. Habib's face had a suppressed smile.

The redness of his face, the drunkenness in his eyes, the agility in his limbs were such that had never been seen before. Habib had taken liberties with Timur several times. It was her awareness as a youth that had made her ignore Timur's status and power.

Then Timur said, 'Habib, I have always agreed with whatever you said. Now, I propose to you something that you will have to agree to.'

Habib bent his head low and said, 'I await your command.'

'Say that you will agree to my proposal.'

'I am your slave, Sire.'

'No, you are the master,' said Timur, 'you are the light of my life. You cannot imagine what I have got from you. I had thought that kingship was the dearest thing and I did everything to get it, even what I should not have done. I stained my hands with the blood of my own people, and also with the blood of the poor. My job is now over. I have laid the foundation. To build on it is now for you. You have to consider yourself the ruler of this country, during my lifetime and after my death.'

As if flying in the sky, Habib said, 'It is a great burden. And my shoulders are not strong enough to bear the weight.'

Entreating, Timur said, 'No, my friend, you will have to accede to my request.'

Habib's eyes brightened, doubts showed on her lips. She said softly, 'I agree.'

'Really!' Extremely happy, Timur said, 'May God give you a long life.'

'If you learn that Habib is an unmarried girl, immature, with half-developed intelligence?'

'She will not only be the ruler of the kingdom, but also the ruler of my heart.'

'Aren't you surprised at what I really am?'

'No, I knew it all along.'

'Since when?'

'Since the time you gazed at me.'

'But you kept it a secret.'

'Yes, but it is you who have taught me all this. Anyway, nobody else here is aware of this.'

'But how did you come to know of it?'

'That I won't tell you,' said Timur with inebriated looks.

And this is the story of Habib, known as Begum Habiba, the wife of Timur.

* * *

No single event constitutes a story, unless it gives expression to some psychological truth. In fact, I don't actually sit down to write a story, till the time I have worked out the outline of the story from the beginning till the end. I also delineate the characters so that they fit in with the story. It is not necessary that the basis of a story should be its readability only. If a story has the psychological climax, the nature of the event to which it relates is immaterial.

Of course, one does sometimes hear of events that provide an easy basis for a short story. But no event can become a story, only because of literary embellishment or a gripping narration. Events exist and so do characters, but it is difficult to find a psychological basis; once it comes up it does not take long to write a short story.

I consider the climax of a story to be an absolute necessity. The climax must also be emotional. It is necessary to build a story in such a way that the climax draws nearer. If, however, an opportunity so presents itself that by exerting one's mind, one can introduce a literary or poetic element, I try to take full advantage of it. This aspect, according to me, is the soul of a short story.

When a story that I write is completed, I read it all over again. If I find some originality, some motivation, some realism, and the power to move, I consider it to be a success. Otherwise, I consider it a failure. I also know only too well that both successful and unsuccessful stories do get into print. In fact, I have seen that very often, a story which I considered a failure, has been appreciated widely by readers and friends alike. I do not therefore consider my yardstick to be a very reliable one.

TWENTY-ONE

AFTER THIRTY YEARS OF WRITINGS, IT IS TIME TO REFLECT ON ART and craft of literature and the literary scene in India.

Short-story literature in Hindi is still in its infancy. Important short story writers are Sudarshan, Kaushik, Jainendra, Ugra, Prasad and Raghuvir. They are the only ones that I can think of. In Jainendra and Ugra, I see a pursuit of originality. Prasad's short stories are creative, but not realistic. Rajeshwari writes well, but the output is limited. Sudarshan's stories are beautiful, but they don't have depth. And Kaushik exaggerates.

It would indeed be appropriate if plots for short stories are taken from actual life, and help resolve the problems of life. I don't think a short story should serve the same purpose as poetry. For, poetry does strike at a chord of the heart more than a short story does. Poetry is written with that purpose. The writer should have the ability to record in his memory such emotions or scenes and use them when the occasion arises...For a writer who is not confident of his memory, it is absolutely necessary to keep a notebook. Writing down in a diary also gives you some practice in writing. Even though I have myself never kept one, I do think it is necessary. For, it is useful to put down in the notebook anything, any unusual face, any enchanting scene. While walking, one gets some ideas or sees new scenes.

Imagination is of greatest importance. It is born out of our observation, it gives more life to writing. Characters drawn from life are much more real.

I never seriously attempted drama. Drama loses its importance when not staged. In fact I never came in touch with drama technique and stagecraft. My dramas were only meant to be read. India has not got a stage, particularly for Hindi or Urdu plays. What passes for stage is the Parsi stage, for which I have a horror. That being so, why should I not stick to my novels where I have greater scope to reveal my characters than I can possibly have in a play. This is why I have preferred the novel as a vehicle of my thought.

Most characters in my novels have been taken from actual life, even though they have been quite veiled... So long as the basis of a character is not real, it remains shadowy and undefined. It does not inspire confidence or faith. In each of my novels – *Premashram, Rangabhoomi* and *Kayakalp* – which were published at intervals of two years each, I have made one character idealistic, with human failings and virtues, but essentially an idealist. In *Premashram* there is Gyan Shankar, in *Rangabhoomi* there is Surdas (*Rangabhoomi* in my opinion, is the best of my works.) And in *Kayakalp* there is Chakradhar. In *Karmabhoomi* there is Amarkant. *Karmabhoomi* has the milieu of the national liberation movement... All great novels have some social pursuit or some great movement as their background. What is Tolstory's *War and Peace* but a history of Napoleon's march on Moscow. But Tolstoy has made the struggle live in his pages. He has introduced characters and incidents which reveal his marvellous insight into human nature. It is the development of character which counts over everything else. If the author is successful in this sphere, he has nothing to fear from criticism. The question is, does the author bring into play the finer and deeper emotions? For, if he does this, no matter what his background, he is dealing with the eternal and deserves to live long.

My ideal of woman is sacrifice, service, purity, all rolled into one. Sacrifice without end, service always ungrudging and purity that of Caesar's wife beyond reproach.

Divorce is common among the proletariat. It is only in the so-called higher classes that this problem has assumed a serious shape. Marriage even at its best, is a sort of compromise and surrender. If a couple mean to be happy, they must be ready to make allowances, while there are people who can never be happy, even under the best of circumstances. In Europe and America, divorces are not uncommon, in spite of all courtship and free intercourse. One of the couple must be ready to bend, male or female does not matter. I refuse to accept that only males are to be blamed. There are cases where ladies created trouble, fancy grievances. When it is not a certainty that divorce will cure our nuptial evils, I don't want to fasten this on society. Of course, there are cases when a divorce becomes a necessity but 'misfit' is in my opinion, nothing but fastidiousness. Divorce without any provision for the poor wife – this demand is only made by morbid individualism. There is no place for it in a society based on equality.

Revolution is the failure of saner methods. I believe in social evolution. My ideal society is one that gives equal opportunities to all. How is that stage to be reached, except by evolution. It is the people's character that is the deciding factor. No social system can flourish, unless we are individually uplifted. What fate a revolution may lead us to, is doubtful. It may lead us to worse forms of dictatorship, denying all personal liberty. I do want to overhaul, but not destroy. If I had some prescience and knew that destruction would lead us to heaven, I would not even mind destroying.

Formerly I believed in a supreme deity, not as a result of thinking, but simply as a traditional belief. That belief is being shattered. Of course, there is a hand behind the universe; but I don't think it has anything to do with human affairs, just as it has nothing to do with the affairs of ants or flies or mosquitoes. The importance, which we have given to ourselves, has no justification.

I have no faith in the other world and so the idea of other-worldliness, which is the greatest killer of youth, does not appeal to me. Of course, there is a healthy youth and a mad youth. A healthy youth consists of a progressive and optimistic view of life; at the same time avoiding the pitfalls. A mad youth consists of rashness and exaggeration of one's own capacities and dreams. I have not ceased to dream and am a bit rash as well. The exaggeration has happily gone. So even of madness I have the better part. I have come to realize that a contented family is a great blessing. And great minds, there are heaps of them. It requires a great deal of judgment to know real greatness from imitation. I cannot imagine a great man rolling in wealth. The moment I see a man rich, all his words of art and wisdom are lost upon me. He seems to me to have submitted to the present social order which is based on the exploitation of the poor by the rich. Any great name not associated with mammon does not attract me. It is quite probable that this frame of mind may be due to my own failure in life. With a handsome credit balance, I might have been just as others are – I could not have resisted the temptation. But I am glad nature and fortune have helped me and my lot is cast with the poor. It gives me spiritual relief. 'Peace within' is my motto.

I am a believer in regular work like Romain Rolland. Life has been to me nothing but work. Even when I was in government service, I devoted my whole time to literary pursuits. I find pleasure in work. There are moments of depression, when money troubles create stress, otherwise I am quite satisfied with my lot. [I have] got more than I deserve.

I don't wish to rest. I am still keen to serve literature and the country. All I need is daal, roti, a tola of ghee, and ordinary clothing. I was never keen to have any wealth nor earn fame. Nor did I aspire to have a bungalow or a motor car. However, I did wish to write a few books of exacting standards and the aim of these books was also to be the freedom of India. I had no aspirations with regard to my two sons. I only wanted them to be honest, truthful and men of determination. I hate the idea of my children being indulgent, wealthy or sycophants.

India can never rise to the highest flights of Art, unless she is murmuring under a foreign yoke. This is where the literature of a subject country is distinguishable from that of a free nation. Our social and political conditions force us to educate ourselves. The greater the feeling, the more didactic the work. Young writers are the greatest sinners in this respect. In their youthful zeal, they forget the principles of art. Are they not excusable?

I wish literature to be masculine. That's why certain poems of Rabindranath Tagore do not appeal to me...Only those verses move me that arouse... Ghalib, of course, I do adore. Bengali literature touches me deeply because it is predominantly feminine. Not much of that type in writing, sentimentalism does affect intellect; it is important arriving at a decision. You need both. Bengalis are sentimental. And sentimentalism can achieve what reasoning or logic can't. The heights that sentimentalism can make one reach is beyond me.

TWENTY-TWO

SEVASADAN WAS FILMED. I GOT RS 750 FOR IT. IF I HADN'T GOT this money when I was in financially difficult straits God knows what my fate would have been. For whenever some money becomes available in straitened circumstances everyone's latent needs raise their heads and become vocal; someone is badly in need of clothes, someone has to get his daughter married. All the money disappears within three or four days.

A film company of Bombay invited me. It wasn't a regular assignment with a monthly salary; it was a contract, Rs 8000 a year. The two options before me were to join them or sell my novels in the market place. Such was my dire need that I could not but accept the offer.

Cinema wants stories that can be staged and should be acceptable to the actors too. For howsoever good a story may be, the actor's suitability is important. Who but a good actor can play the role? I don't consider the mystery element to be important. The theme of the two stories that I had written was somewhat commonplace.

The world of cinema is entirely a new field. They wanted stories for pictures that are romantic and sensational, and they wanted me to write stories without reference to the frame that I have. I have gone so far as I could to accommodate the director's wishes...I had to do it. Idealism is exacting, and often one has to sideline it...

Cinema is no place for a literary person. I came to this line as it offered some chance of getting financially independent, but now I see I was under a delusion and am going back to my literature. I regard literary works as the aim of my life. Cinema is only what leadership might have meant for me, only healthier.

From Bombay I went to Madras, and then on to Mysore and Bangalore. I am keen to write about my travels in the south. But I haven't kept any notes. I will therefore have to write from memory.

I was pleased to see that Hindi was making rapid strides there. Those who cannot take part in the liberation movement were involved in learning the Rashtrabhasha. This part of the country is really enchanting. Most people are interested in the arts of singing and dancing. Every mohalla has women's organizations and almost all of them hold classes in Hindi.

I sat there, garlanded. It was there that I felt the weakness of not being able to speak in public. People there looked forward to see what the great writer would say. And there I was, not knowing what to say. But I must say, the trip was enjoyable.

How much did I get from Bombay? Only Rs 6,300. Of this amount, my sons took Rs 1500, and my daughter Rs 400; the press took about Rs 500. My stay in Bombay for over ten months cost me at least Rs 2,500. Thus I brought back Rs 1400. Not a single one of the hopes I had entertained when I went to Bombay seems to have been realized. The film producers were not willing to deviate even an inch from the path which they had so far been treading to produce their films. They equate vulgarity with what they call entertainment value. They believe in the unusual, in kings and queens and conspiracies being hatched by their ministers, in fake encounters, public kissing. All these are their tools. I wrote some sociological stories which the educated classes would have liked to see, but the producers are sceptical about the success of such films.

Back in Banaras, *Godan* was completed and published. However, there was to be little rest. There was the itch to travel. What was needed was to propagate Hindustani instead of Urdu and also the creation of a national forum for the regional languages of India and the foundation of the Bharatiya Sahitya Parishad. I also needed to take steps to see that the concept got strength.

Today we are familiar with the works of British authors. Even the names of well-known French and German writers are on our fingertips. But we are not at all aware of the writers of our own regional languages. In order to remove ignorance and in order to introduce their works, we endeavoured to lay the foundation of an organization whose first task would be to bring out a journal which would carry the literary works from all the Indian languages through the medium of Hindi. Until now there has been no such thing as Indian literature. From time to time every province tries to promote its own literature. The writers of one province don't know what exists in the literature of other languages. Very few Urdu writers know what appears in Bengali or Gujarati, Marathi or Tamil and Kannada. Similarly also there is complete ignorance about Urdu literature in these provinces.

Under the chairmanship of Mahatma Gandhi, the Bharatiya Sahitya Parishad came into being. *Hans* was handed over to the Parishad so that it became the Parishad's mouthpiece. I travelled to

Lahore to address the Arya Pratinidhi Sabha. I presided over the Progressive Writers Association's convention at Lucknow and the Hindustani Sabha at New Delhi and Aligarh.

(Since January 1936) I was in bed, suffering from gastric ulcers. I vomitted blood. My treatment brought little relief. I was no longer associated with *Hans* which had become a headache for me. The baniyas who now controlled it charged me for overspending on *Hans*. I had put my heart and soul in this venture, worked single handedly and had spent time and put in labour. But they were oblivious of all this. I had given *Hans* to the Bharatiya Sahitya Parishad in the fond hope that it would continue to be printed in my (Saraswati) press. However, they later decided to bring it out under the auspices of the Sasta Sahitya Mandal of Delhi. The Parishad would thus be saving Rs 50 a month. I was happy because the literature that *Hans* was propagating was like the Bhakti literature of the Mahajani culture of which there is plenty in Hindi.

* * *

Now in the evening of life, it seems apt to think and ponder over the basic issues of present-day Mahajani culture and to sum up in last testament. I did this in my last essay in the last issue of Hans.

What is Mahajan culture? What is its background? Strong muscles and a stout heart were the principal requisites of life in the feudal civilization. The corresponding instruments in the hands of imperialism were the qualities of head, speech and a semblance of willingness to carry out orders. The two social orders, along with their faults, had some good qualities too. Man had not lost all his goodness. If the feudal lord wanted to quench his thirst he could also stake his life for the sake of a friend or a benefactor. If the monarch considered his orders to be law and never tolerated insolence, he also gave shelter to his subjects and dispensed justice.

His invasion of other's dominions was either to take revenge for an insult or to establish his supremacy. He might also have been inspired with a brave man's ideas of expending his domination. The reason for this attitude was that the monarchs and kings considered the general mass of people to be the fuel for their mill of self-interest and the wish to amass wealth. They shared the joys and sorrows of their subjects.

The object of every single action in the Mahajan's civilization is only to accumulate wealth. If it subjugates another country, it is to benefit its moneylenders and capitalists. It would seem the world is ruled by moneylenders. Mankind is split into two sections. While by far the bigger section is that of the exploited, the smaller is that of people with power and influence who dictate to the latter. It has little sympathy with the lot of the bigger section. The latter exists only to sweat for the masters, and then disappears unsung, unmourned and unlamented. What is still more painful is that the ideas of the exploited class have taken root among the exploited, with the result that every man now considers himself to be a hunter and the society his prey. He considers his identity separate from that of society. In fact, the only link is that he would fool society and derive maximum benefit from it.

Greed has completely overshadowed all that was good and important in man. Today the only test for a good upbringing and nobility of character is money. He who has money is considered a superman. He may be evil at heart. But literature, art and music will bow before one who is rich. The atmosphere is so vitiated that it is becoming difficult to exist in it. Doctors will not look at you unless you pay them hefty fees. Lawyers and barristers weigh their minutes in gold sovereigns. The success of character and competence is adjudged from their monetary value. The maulvi and the Brahmin are also the slaves of those with money. The press too sings praises of those with money. Money has so overpowered the head and heart of man that it appears difficult to assault its domain. Man, the very epitome of love, mercy, nobility and truthfulness, has become a machine, devoid of all compassion and affection.

The Mahajani civilization has evolved new rules and conventions which today have become the base of our society. One of these rules is that 'Time means Money.' In the earlier phases of human history, time meant life, and its best use was for the acquisition of knowledge and for helping the poor. Its best use now is to earn. When the doctor puts his hand on the pulse of the patient, his eye is on the watch. If the patient gives the doctor only one sovereign, the doctor won't give more than a minute. The patient may be dying to tell his tale of pain, but the doctor is inattentive and unconcerned. In his eyes, the patient's value lies only in the fact that he pays him a fee. He would give the prescription and move on to the next patient. A teacher teaches his class, but the duration of the class is fixed. And he keeps a clock before him. He gets up to leave, irrespective of whether or not the day's lesson has been completed. How can he give the class more time than is allotted? Time is money.

The greed for money has disgraced man and also the friendliness in man. Not just of relations, today a husband does not have time to even converse with wives or children. He thinks the time he devotes to conversation would be better devoted to some other work. The only justification of life is to make money. The rest is all a waste of time. He spends time perforce on food and sleep; for it is not possible to live without them.

Should one of your friends or relations earn fame in his own home town, you can take it that you would not be welcome there. And if you do go to his house, you will have to send in your visiting card. The gentleman would have lots of work and with great difficulty would give you a few minutes or would tell you frankly that he is not free the whole day. He is a worshipper of money and has bade goodbye to friendship. If you are involved in a legal suit and have a lawyer friend, don't expect any help from him; he may not talk of his fee but he would not pay any attention to your case either. It would be far better if you go to someone not known to you and pay his fees for when someone attains a position in anything, he loses the last trace of humanity and every minute of his life is equated with money.

Greed for the acquisition of wealth should not be allowed to go so far as to drive out the sentiments of humanity, friendship, affection and sympathy.

You cannot, of course, condemn everyone who is a slave to money. When the entire world goes in that direction, one has to follow. Honour and position have been the highest of man's ambitions. When the acquisition of knowledge was the instrument of honour and position, men went after it. When money is the only instrument for the attainment of honour and respect, man is forced to worship it with a single-minded devotion. Time, to a successful man, is money. When one sees that another achieves success this way, one too follows in the footsteps of the successful one. And who can blame him? Greed for respect and honour cannot be erased from man's heart. He sees that he who has no money – and not because he does not recognize that time is money – is not bothered about it, even though he may be a master of his art. Anyone with the least zest for life will find this position of callousness unbearable. He would have to lose himself in the worship of the goddess of wealth. Only then will she bless him. And this devotion is not casual; it is paramount. His mind now functions in a way that he is not attached to anything but the accumulation of wealth. All his mental, religious and cultural interests are now focussed on one thing – money. This is particularly so because he sees that none except the money is his own, that affectionate friends come to him for their own selfish ends, that his relatives worship nothing but his money. He knows that were he a poor man, relatives would never have come to him. He has to carve a place for himself in society, to save a little for his old age, to provide for his children so that they don't have to suffer. He has an experience of this stern world and doesn't wish his children to go through situations which put a damper on all ambitions. He will have to pass through all the stages alone and without making business the basis of life, he would not be able to pass even one stage.

The other motto of this civilization is 'Business is Business' and there in no place for sentiment in it. The old rule of life did not have the bluntness which may be termed shame-facedness. The latter in fact is the soul of the new rule of life. In the mutual give and take of financial transactions, there is no place for courtesy or humanity. How can you have friendship in business? When someone takes shelter behind this new principle, you are speechless: A gentleman in great difficulty is forced to go to a moneylender and wishes him to help him out. He hopes that he may reduce the rate of interest. And when he sees that the friend talks in the usual business vein, he requests him for a little concession and brings tears of mercy and appeals to him saying, 'I am in great difficulty at the moment and would not have bothered you otherwise.' He is cut short and is told in the manner of an order, 'you forget that Business is Business'. The person making a request is crestfallen. He accepts all the conditions of his friend who worships the principles of business.

Of all the conventions introduced by the Mahajani civilization in this world, the most fatal and the most parasitic sucking is of 'Business is Business'. Business between husband and wife! Business between father and son! Business between teacher and pupil! All the intellectual and social bonds of man melt into thin air. If today there is any relationship between man and man, it is that of business.

If, unfortunately, a girl is unmarried until late in her life, and is unable to earn her livelihood, she becomes a servant in her father's house. Not that boys and girls don't work in the house, but then they are not considered paid servants. In this civilization, however, an unmarried girl after a certain age becomes the servant of the brothers. The revered father also becomes a servant of the son! And so does the mother who gave birth to the son! One's own relative are nowhere. A brother becomes a guest in a brother's house.

The soul of this pawnshop civilization is individualism. One becomes selfish for oneself only. The same desire for respect and honour, the same worry for the future, the question of provision for the future for the wife and the children, the same exhibitionism and the same necessity to impress others. These then are the principal worries of everyone and these cannot be done away with. Anyone who does not obey the rules and conventions of this civilization will find his future dark.

Till now there was no way other than to follow the rules and conventions of this civilization. One had to bow down to this. The moneylender went about arrogantly and the entire world kowtowed to him. The king was his own, the ministers were his slaves, and he was the master, holding the keys to war or peace. The world was at his beck and call. And he was supreme.

But now the sun of a new civilization has arisen in the Far West. This has uprooted this spectacular Mahajani civilization. The fundamental principle of this new civilization is that the individual who, through his manual or mental labours, can produce something is to be the most honoured citizen of the State, and he who goes about living upon the earnings of his ancestors, or on the labours of others, is the lowest of all. He doesn't have the right to exercise his vote for the administration of the country. Nor is he entitled to the right of citizenship.

The moneylender is nervous. They are running down this new civilization and are cursing it. And this is being portrayed as fatal to individual freedom, liberty of religious beliefs and of following the dictates of one's conscience. All sorts of allegations are being levelled and all sorts of black spots are being discovered. It is being portrayed in the most vicious form. Through the use of all the media available to people with resources, a great propaganda is being carried on against this civilization. But truth penetrates through all this darkness and illuminates the way.

Without any doubt, this new civilization has broken the claws and blunted the teeth of the so-called individualistic freedom. In the new social order, no millionaire can fatten himself on the blood of hundreds of thousands of labourers. He is not free to increase the prices of articles of everyday use for his own profit, nor to start wars for the propagation of his industrial produce, nor to ensure the suppression of weaker nations through manufacturing instruments of war. If therein lies freedom it is certainly not freedom according to the values of the new civilization.

Freedom means airy houses, healthy food, clean villages, centres for recreation and physical culture, electric lights and fans, easy justice for all, then the liberty and freedom that obtain in this new social order are not obtained in even the most civilized nation. If religious freedom means to follow the vicious preachings of the parasitical Brahmins, missionaries and mullahs and the traditions of age-old blind faith, such freedom is certainly conspicuous by its absence. If freedom of belief means social service, human sympathy, sacrifice of the individual for the larger good of the community, good actions, purity of body and mind, then the freedom of good behaviour that obtains in this new civilization has not been seen anywhere.

In a social order where there are inequalities of wealth, we find that jealousy, coercion, compulsion, force, dishonesty, untruth, untenable accusations, prostitution, loose morals and all other evils are necessarily present. When there is not too much of wealth, and where large masses of people live alike, why should there be jealousies and the use of force? Why should there be fraudulent cases, burglaries, dacoities, and moral crimes? All these evils are the result of wealth. It is the Mahajani civilization that has created them, that nourishes them, and it is that civilization which wishes that the downtrodden, sick and the exploited should consider them as heavenly dispensation and resign themselves to it. If they show the least signs of revolt, there are the police to crush them, the law courts to punish them and exile or push them out. Money brings in its train all those evils. But mere pruning, without cutting at the root, would be a waste of effort. The new civilization considers the wealthy as low. If anyone lives in a grand style, he is considered mean and deserving of contempt. No woman becomes beautiful by putting on ornaments; in fact she becomes an object of derision. To live in a style which is higher than that of the common run of people is considered vulgar. For to get inebriated is considered evil not from a religious point of view but from the viewpoint of correct social behaviour, for drunkenness ends courage in man, his forbearance and capacity to work.

This social order has not given the individual the freedom to make the large mass of people the instruments of the fulfilment of one's aspirations, to benefit, on one pretext or the other, from the labours of others, or to manœuver high government posts with salaries. Highly placed government officials in the new order get as much as a skilled workman. He does not live in skyscrapers, but lives in three or four rooms. His wife does not go about like a princess distributing prizes in schools, but does either manual work or an assignment in a newspaper. By government service the husband does not consider himself to be the monarch of all that he surveys, but only a servant.

August 1936: For the last one and a half months, I was suffering from inflammation of the liver. I vomitted a massive amount of blood. As there was little improvement in my health in Banaras, I went to Lucknow for treatment under Dr Hargovind Sahai. Blood tests were carried out. Many other tests were to be done before the doctor could diagnose the malady and decide on the treatment. I cannot eat, nor can I digest anything. Either there is some improvement, or this is going to be the end for me.

(*The end came on 8 October 1936*)